VIRTUALLY OBSCENE

VIRTUALLY OBSCENE

The Case for an Uncensored Internet

Amy E. White

Foreword by Nadine Strossen

$$V = k(G)^{\circ}$$

McFarland & Company, Inc., Publishers
Jefferson, North Carolina, and London

LIBRARY OF CONGRESS CATALOGUING-IN-PUBLICATION DATA

White, Amy E., 1974–
  Virtually obscene : the case for an uncensored internet / Amy E.
White ; foreword by Nadine Strossen.
      p.   cm.
  Includes bibliographical references and index.

  ISBN-13: 978-0-7864-2801-4
  ISBN-10: 0-7864-2801-5
  (softcover : 50# alkaline paper) ∞

  1. Internet pornography.   2. Intellectual freedom.   3. Censorship — United States.   I. Title.
HQ471.W45   2006
363.4'702854678 — dc22   2006028076

British Library cataloguing data are available

©2006 Amy E. White. All rights reserved

Cover illustration ©2006 Photodisc

Manufactured in the United States of America

McFarland & Company, Inc., Publishers
  Box 611, Jefferson, North Carolina 28640
  www.mcfarlandpub.com

For Alexander

Acknowledgments

I first became interested in Internet regulation and censorship while completing my graduate work at Bowling Green State University. Without the help of Loren Lomasky, Kathleen Dixon, Daniel Jacobson and Walter Maner this manuscript would not be possible. Nadine Strossen's work has inspired me, and I thank her for her words of encouragement and her excellent foreword. Finally, I would like to thank my family for their patience and insight. Particularly, I am grateful to Allen White. Without Allen, I would not be on the path I am on today.

Contents

Foreword

In *Virtually Obscene: The Case for an Uncensored Internet*, Amy White lays out the compelling rationales for protecting freedom of speech, including sexually oriented expression, and she shows why these rationales are especially pertinent and powerful in cyberspace. Correspondingly, White analyzes and rebuts the justifications that are offered by government officials and others who seek to censor cyberspeech, and in particular sexually oriented cyberspeech.

White cogently refutes the proffered rationales for subjecting sexually oriented cyberspeech to greater restraints than the Supreme Court has upheld for sexually oriented expression in other media. Moreover, she makes a strong case against the obscenity exception that the Supreme Court has carved out of the First Amendment, persuasively arguing that this obscenity exception should certainly not be extended to cyberspace. White's analysis is a welcome defense of an uncensored Internet, consistent with values of free speech and individual autonomy more generally.

To be sure, in the landmark 1997 case of *Reno v. ACLU*, the Supreme Court struck down the first federal cybercensorship law, and held that cyberspeech is entitled to the same high level of First Amendment protection as that accorded to print material; the Court rejected the government's argument that cyberspeech should receive instead only the reduced protection that the Court traditionally has accorded to the highly regulated broadcast media. However, Congress promptly passed two other cybercensorship laws, one of which the Supreme Court upheld, and the second of which is still being litigated in a case now entitled *Gonzales v. ACLU.* As the two cited case names indicate, cyber-censorship laws are politically popular and strongly defended by too many elected officials, ranging across the political spectrum: from President Bill Clinton and his attorney general, Janet Reno, to President George W. Bush and his attorney general, Alberto Gonzales.

I am proud that the American Civil Liberties Union has taken the lead in defending freedom of online expression, just as we have been in the forefront of the free speech cause since our founding in 1920. I am also proud that we presciently founded a "Cyberliberties Taskforce" substantially before most people had even heard of the Internet, and that we have won many historic court rulings, as well as some key legislative battles, which have helped to maintain the Internet as a free speech zone. However, as the ACLU's principal founder, Roger Baldwin, astutely observed: "No fight for civil liberties ever stays won." This insight certainly rings true in the cyber context, especially considering the constant political pressures from Democratic and Republican politicians alike, as noted above. In the crucial ongoing struggle to maintain online free expression, Amy White's fine book provides strong and needed support.

Nadine Strossen
President of the American Civil Liberties Union
March 2, 2006

Introduction

Compared to the rise of other communications technologies, the Internet has expanded at a phenomenal rate. In its wake there are many questions yet to be solved. One of the most discussed is regulation of sexually explicit material on the Internet. While there are many forms that regulation can take, in this book I will only address the question of state-sponsored regulation that focuses on the illegalization of sexually explicit materials. Proponents of regulating material in this fashion often appeal to the potential of material on the Internet to cause harm. On the other hand, proponents of an unregulated Internet often appeal to the First Amendment of the United States Constitution or a similar right to free speech in order to justify a special protected status for speech.[1] As popular as both of these strategies are, I believe they fail to philosophically justify either argument adequately. The focus of this manuscript will be to prove the failure of the two aforementioned strategies and offer a third alternative.

Dangerous Speech

> *Unabridged dictionaries are dangerous books. In their pages man's evilest thoughts find means of expression. Terms denoting all that is foul or blasphemous or obscene are printed there for men, women and children to read and ponder. Such books should have their covers pad-locked and be chained to reading desks, in the custody of responsible librarians, preferably church members in good standing. Permission to open such books should be granted only after careful inquiry as to which word a reader plans to look up, and how he plans to use it.* — Deacon Ephraim Stebbins[2]

Arguments for the regulation of certain forms of expression have been used extensively throughout history and appear in Book Ten of Plato's *Republic*. Often the underlying idea behind these historical arguments and current versions is the same: some expression is dangerous in the wrong hands. Plato pointed out this danger when he referred to writing as a *pharmokon*.[3] In the *Phaedrus* he argues that writing, which was the newest communication medium at the time, was dangerous and would cause a degradation of the community. Plato gave many reasons why he believed this would occur. One such reason is illustrated when Plato writes of a myth, most likely devised by Plato, of Thamus and Theuth. According to this myth, Thamus (the Greek name for the god Ammon) was king of Egypt and was presented with an idea by Theuth, the Egyptian god of writing and mathematics, who had recently invented writing.[4] Theuth presents writing to Thamus under the pretext that it is a potion[5] for memory and wisdom.[6] Thamus, however, rejects the invention and maintains that it will, in fact, aid forgetfulness. This is because those who use it will put their trust in it and rely less on their own memory to retain knowledge. Also, it is Thamus' claim that writing will give only a sample of something to its readers without properly teaching them and will, in turn, create the illusion of knowing. Thus, the readers will appear wise but, in actuality, not be.[7] This, it is argued, will make for a society of arrogant and relatively unknowledgeable persons. In other words, writing has the power to transform personalities and transform society. This is echoed in Book Ten of Plato's *Republic* where all poets are thrown out of Plato's city because their work has such an effectual power. While the harms claimed to occur are varied, modern arguments take almost exactly the same form as those in Plato's *Phaedrus* and *The Republic*.

One writer to point out the negative effects of a modern communication medium, the television, is Neil Postman. Postman, using an argument almost identical to Plato's, argues against the rise of television in his book *Amusing Ourselves to Death: Public Discourse in the Age of Show Business*.[8] The basic structure of the argument changes little from Plato's critique of writing to Postman's critique of television. Postman and Plato point out the empirical fact that what we can communicate in a culture is limited by the methods of communication used.

One example Postman uses is that of smoke signals, through which it is quite unlikely that intricate philosophical arguments could, in any reasonable way, be communicated. The next step of the argument advances the idea that it is quite possible that, as Postman writes, "two media so vastly different cannot accommodate the same ideas."[9] The next premise is something to the effect that, given the first two premises, with a new, prevalent form of communication, some ideas cannot be expressed. This leads to the conclusion that some ideas will be less available to the culture or persons communicating in this new fashion. Therefore, the shift to a new form of communication, in a sense, transforms thinking by giving prominence to some ideas over others. It is then possible that what we believe and who we are as persons are linked closely to our forms of expression.[10] Thus, new communications methods have the power to drastically affect persons and, according to Postman and Plato, cause them (and society in general) harm. This is, perhaps, why *logos*[11] is to be feared by Plato as a drug[12] that persuades people to believe they know the truth of things when they do not.[13]

Given the potential power of a new communication method, with every new communication medium the question of regulation will likely occur. From the invention of the written word to Gutenberg's movable press in 1455, to the Internet, as more information becomes available and widely circulates there will be pressures aimed at regulation. Thus, in a sense, this manuscript merely adds a new chapter to an already written book. J.S. Mill recognized this when he commenced his discussion on free speech in *On Liberty* with an apology. Mill writes, "[T]hose to whom nothing which I am about to say will be new, may therefore, I hope, excuse me, if on a subject which for now three centuries has been so often discussed, I venture on one discussion more."[14]

I also must beg the readers' indulgence for beginning still another discussion of freedom of speech and regulation. However, while historical arguments concerning regulation and free speech are, in and of themselves, interesting, a new twist is added when they are applied to a global medium such as the Internet. The Internet is unlike anything that has come before. While the individual parts can be compared and reduced to more traditional media, the whole is often greater than the sum of the parts. The Internet has the potential to have an enormous impact on the lives of many persons in many nations. While it is true that other communications methods have had great impact, the Internet is unique. Because of the Internet's global nature, speed and versatility, questions arising from its use will also be unique in many ways.[15]

The importance of this project can, perhaps, best be illustrated through the words of Alexander Meiklejohn. Meiklejohn writes:

> When this new form of communication became available, there opened up before us the possibility that, as a people living a common life under a common agreement, we might communicate with one another freely with regard to the values, the opportunities, the difficulties, the joys and sorrows, the hopes and fears, the plans and purposes, of that common life. It seemed possible that, amid all our differences, we might become a community of mutual understanding and of shared interests. It was that hope which justified our making the radio "free," our giving it the protection of the First Amendment.[16]

However, Meiklejohn is soon to point out that that radio is not free when he writes, "Never was a human hope more bitterly disappointed."[17] While it may seem odd to compare the Internet to radio there are many commonalties. When radio was in its infancy it was a decentralized technology where amateurs could broadcast any content they wished. Also, radio equipment was inexpensive and readily available.[18] However, soon the question came about as to its future, the same dilemma that confronts us now. The Internet, just like radio or even television, has enormous potential. In a world where money often buys the right to be heard, the Internet may have the potential to level the playing field in some respects. The Internet may be a forum where the average person with a flair for web design can attract as many listeners as a major corporation. It has the potential to restore a town meeting type of atmosphere and allow citizens to organize in virtual communities. However, just as Meiklejohn's hopes were dissolved with the radio, the potential of the Internet could leave us bitterly disappointed. This work is perhaps a step towards avoiding such consequences.

An Outline

The manuscript is organized into seven main chapters. Chapter 1 provides background information on attempts to regulate sexually explicit[19] materials and briefly outline the development of the Internet. This section introduces the reader to current attempts at regulation of such materials and the methods involved. I also, in this section, differentiate the Internet from other communications methods and detail the unique and complex nature of the Internet. It is my hope that this section will serve as a compass that will afford the reader an orientation needed to navigate the body of the book.

Chapter 2 evaluates the current regulation of obscenity on the Internet. In this chapter, a detailed argument is provided to the effect that an obscenity standard, based on community standards, should not be used to regulate the Internet. Given this, I conclude that the current standard used in such regulation, which is community based, is unworkable.

Chapter 3 investigates the claim that the Internet should not be regulated in the United States due to the protection afforded by the First Amendment of the United States Constitution and the value of free speech. This chapter, titled "Why Free Speech Alone Should Not Protect Internet Obscenity and Pornography," is, perhaps, the most ambitious in the book. In this chapter I not only examine the claims that opponents of Internet regulation make but also the applicability of the First Amendment to Internet speech. I argue that proponents' claims, which are often based on the arguments originally expounded by John Stuart Mill, fall short and are not sound. While this step is, in itself, ambitious, I further argue that the First Amendment should not apply to most of the content that proponents of Internet regulation target. I advance an approach similar to that advocated by Alexander Meiklejohn and divide speech into two distinct categories: public and private.

In Chapter 4, I examine the argument made by many proponents of Internet regulation that an unregulated Internet will be harmful to children.[20] Proponents of the harm to children argument claim that children can be harmed by an unregulated Internet in several ways. This argument has been used extensively in proposals to regulate the Internet in the United States. Common claims offered to support this argument are that children can gain access to questionable materials,[21] gain access to information that lets them do questionable things and can be targeted by Internet pedophiles. In this chapter I examine each of these claims and argue that they are defective. It is my conclusion that the harm to children argument cannot justify Internet content regulation. In short, the harm that proponents of the argument claim will occur will either not occur or not be sufficient to justify regulation.

Chapter 5, "Harm to Women," is similar to Chapter 4; however, the argument of concern is that an unregulated Internet harms women. The harm to women argument is really a subset of the larger claims that the availability of pornography, in general, harms women and that regulation reduces such availability and harm. A 2002 estimate concluded that there existed over 400,000 commercial pornography websites worldwide.[22] Because the Internet contains such large quantities[23] of pornographic material that is relatively easily accessed,[24] pornography is harmful to women, an uncensored Internet surely advances such harm. Therefore, because advancing harm could be a harm in itself, an unregulated Internet is harmful to women. Claims that pornography is harmful to women advanced by authors such as Catharine Mackinnon, Andrea Dworkin and many others are extensive. Proponents of the harm to women arguments claim that there are many ways such harm occurs. Common arguments claim that Internet pornography libels women, degrades women, denies women positive liberties and that the women involved in the production of pornography are assaulted and abused. In this chapter, I scrutinize each of these claims and argue that they, like those given in support of the harm to children argument, are not strong and should not be used to justify Internet regulation.

Chapter 6 examines yet another argument to the effect that an unregulated Internet is harmful. This chapter, "Harm to the Moral Environment and Offense," examines the arguments made by proponents of regulation that the Internet erodes societal morals and causes extreme offense. Many United States senators and other advocates of governmental regulation regularly express this claim. I approach this chapter by noting the similarity of this argument to the argument made by Patrick Devlin in the famous Hart/Devlin debate.[25] The failures in Devlin's argument are also prevalent in the current reincarnation of the argument. The defects present in these arguments are unlikely to be overcome. Given the faults of both arguments, I conclude that the harm to morals argument does not justify Internet regulation.

Drawing on the conclusions offered in previous chapters, I offer in Chapter 7 a consequentialist argument for the existence of an unregulated Internet. Given that, as concluded in previous chapters, the arguments advanced to prove that sexually explicit Internet materials are harmful fail, there will be little utility gained by regulation. In addition, in this chapter I outline the harm that will be produced by regulating the Internet and conclude that, overall, disutility will ensue if sexually explicit Internet materials are regulated.

1

The Unknown Territory
and the Quest to
Tame the Internet Beast

*Governments of the Industrial World, you weary giants of flesh and steel,
I come from Cyberspace, the new home of the Mind. On behalf of the
future, I ask you of the past to leave us alone, you are not welcome among
us. You have no sovereignty where we gather.* — John Perry Barlow[1]

Introduction

"Live Sex Shows," "XXX," and "Cum On In," are just a few of the
slogans displayed on numerous websites. These sites display, sometimes
for a fee, sexually explicit material. This material ranges from fairly common sexual acts between adults to bestiality and fetishes. If one looks
hard enough, he or she can find almost any type of sexually explicit material on the Internet, including nudity, pictures and descriptions of intercourse between both heterosexual and homosexual partners, bestiality, live
sex shows via web cameras, sex chat, child pornography,[2] simulated
child pornography, and even furniture pornography.[3] Not only are such
materials available on the Internet but, in some cases, they can be accessed
by just a few clicks of a mouse button. Furthermore, the Internet takes
information transfer to a new level by allowing users to chat as if they
were on a telephone, making sites available to read and view as one
would a book, allowing the use of video plug-ins to show films and
produce live feeds and much more. In short, the Internet transmits mate-

11

rial that is offensive or considered harmful to a large population through a multifaceted array of connections at speeds previously unattainable. This ability of the Internet is examined in a Scottish proposal to regulate extreme pornography. The proposal states, "[T]his material has never been available so easily or in such quantity. In pre-internet days, individuals who wished to view this kind of material would need to seek it out, bring it into their home or have it delivered in physical form as magazines, videos, photographs etc., risking discovery and embarrassment at every stage."[4] In addition to the speed and privacy the Internet provides a user wishing to view such material, the anatomy of the Internet is unique and, perhaps, impossible to regulate effectively.

With the existence of pornography and obscenity on the Internet, a market has developed around gaining access to this material. Currently, pages containing adult oriented material are one of the biggest traffic generators on the Internet. One of the largest of such sites, www.whitehouse.com, is a publicly traded stock. However, even with (perhaps because of) their popularity, sites featuring this material have been the topic of intense debate. Many countries, including the United States, have tried to enact laws to regulate Internet obscenity and pornography. These regulations aim at controlling Internet content in ways much like other communications mediums are regulated. The fact that offending speech is technologically dispersed instantaneously to millions of potential recipients in the privacy of their own homes strengthens the impetus to regulate.

The purpose of this chapter is to examine what exactly the Internet consists of, explain how the Internet is different from previous regulated communications technology and outline regulatory attempts and possible avenues for regulation. This will be done in an attempt to set a foundation for arguments in further chapters. However, I also hope to illustrate in this chapter how different the Internet is from any previously existing communications technology.

The Internet: History and Structure

Contrary to a popular misconception, the Internet is more than just access to the World Wide Web; it involves a wide variety of communication and information retrieval processes. Paul Baran, a Rand Corporation researcher, conceptualized the basic framework for the Internet. Baran wanted to answer the question of how United States officials could communicate in the aftermath of nuclear war. Baran developed the idea of a decentralized communications network that lacked main hubs and precise points of vulnerability. However, Baran's theory was not realized until 1969 when a group of engineers working for the federal government's Advanced Research Projects Agency (ARPA)[5] started building such a network. This network was called ARPAnet.[6]

Many authors have described in detail the events leading to the rise of the Internet from the ARPAnet military structure.[7] While the Internet has features similar to those of other communication methods, it is unique in many ways. The Internet is not a tangible device; no one entity manufactures or produces it and it is not owned or controlled by any government or corporation. The Internet's survival simply depends on the computer networks used and established by people all over the world. It operates by connecting millions of computer networks and host computers or international high-capacity "backbone"[8] systems to each other. The computers which form the Internet are connected by many different methods. Some of these methods include fiber optic cable, twisted-pair copper wire, wireless signals and other methods. The information traveling on these networks is translated by a computer into a universal protocol called TCP/IP, which uses a common name and enables other computers connected to the network to find and understand the information. It is these protocols that really define the network. The machines that talk to one another using IP and their connections *are* the Internet.

On the Internet, information can travel from computer to computer along paths called routers. This is a packet switching network. In other words, it breaks information into packets of bits that can be transmitted as capacity allows. Each packet is labeled with the address of its final destination. Information in these packets will switch routers when it can no longer use the current path to deliver the information. This is one respect in which the Internet is unlike other communications media that tie up entire channels during transmission. The Internet has a plethora of routers. Thus, if any path breaks down, the packets will take alternative routes to reach their destinations, where they are reassembled by the recipient machine.[9] There is no centralized control of the packet routing on the Internet. Each computer independently coordinates information traffic with its nearest connected neighbors. Each of these independently acting computers has a systems administrator. Thus, there is no central authority and the system as a whole does not depend on the functioning of any individual node.

Until recently there were three aspects of the Internet that were the subject of concern for regulators: electronic mail (e-mail), automatic mailing list services and the World Wide Web.[10] As stated in *Reno v. ACLU*, "[T]aken together, these tools constitute a unique medium — known to its users as cyberspace — located in no particular geographical location but available to anyone, anywhere in the world, with access to the Internet."[11] The list given by the Court is outdated, and there are currently many methods by which obscene or sexually explicit material can be passed using the Internet. These include the avenues mentioned by the Court as well as peer-to-peer (P2P) file sharing, instant messaging (IM), Usenet, computer bulletin board systems (BBSs), Internet Relay Chat (IRC), downloading materials to portable devices and many others.

E-mail is one of the most popular features of the Internet and basically involves transmitting information from one account to another. This is the fast, electronic equivalent of a postal carrier delivering mail to a specified address. However, no postal carrier is needed and, due to the nature of the Internet, a letter's route cannot be traced while being transferred to its final destination. Also, many times, it is possible for both the sender and receiver to remain anonymous, thus, the mail cannot be interrupted in route, at the source or at the final destination. E-mail can be viewed on a computer, some cellular phones and a plethora of hand-held devices. Many types of files can also be transmitted by e-mail as attachments.

The World Wide Web (WWW) organizes information on the Internet. The information is organized on websites that have "addresses" that allow users of the World Wide Web to exchange information. A user of the World Wide Web utilizes a web browser[12] which incorporates the web's pointer standard, the Universal Resource Locator (URL), to locate a particular website. Every document on the web has a unique URL and any user can create a "homepage" with his or her own URL. This allows all other users to virtually visit their web "address." While there are many "addresses" that contain sexually explicit material, such material is also passed on the Internet in many less familiar ways.

An avenue of communication on the Internet is Usenet. While Usenet has declined in popularity, it is still available and active. Howard Rheingold writes of Usenet that it is an "anarchic, unkillable, censorship-resistant, aggressively noncommercial, voraciously growing conversation among millions of people in dozens of countries."[13] The character of Usenet is due in part to the way the system is designed. Anyone with access to the network can send out an individual posting to the rest of Usenet. To route a message, Usenet uses a topic, or newsgroup, instead of an individual or mailing list. There is a Usenet newsgroup for just about any topic and I, as an individual, can join the discussion merely by posting my message. When a person reads my message he or she can post one in reply to the entire newsgroup, mail me directly or disregard my message. If a user does not like my message or is not interested in the topics I post, he or she can filter out future messages from me. This structure creates a vast informal network where every reader can post and also communicate with other readers privately. Again, there is no central governing hierarchy on Usenet.

Today, Usenet does have some rules, but they are only in the form of norms. If a user breaks one of these norms they usually receive angry e-mail, are flamed[14] or are filtered by users. Howard Rheingold calls Usenet "a giant coffeehouse" and a "worldwide digital version of the Speaker's Corner in Hyde Park, an unedited collection of letters to the editor."[15] It is mass media because every piece of information posted has the potential to reach millions, but it is much different from conventional mass media because every user has the ability to reply or create his or her own posting. In most conventional media only a small number of people have the power to determine what information is available.

Computer bulletin board systems (BBSs) were one of the first forms of Internet communication and are still used today. Bulletin board systems allow users to post information on many electronic bulletin boards or even start their own board. The discussion on the boards is similar to that on Usenet. In many ways the practical differences between the systems are in name only. However, there are some technical differences. Bulletin board systems are usually linked to the Internet by gateways but they need not be. Any personal computer running BBS software with a modem can operate a bulletin board system. Just post the telephone number on some operating BBS and a crowd will soon develop. People can call your BBS (or enter by the Net) and leave private messages or public information. Also, a BBS owner can start a business by posting information that users can only access after paying a fee.

Chatting is also a popular method to communicate over the Internet. Sometimes chat rooms are linked to WWW websites or e-mail. Users can also chat utilizing instant messaging programs (IM) or in gaming environments. Many Internet users communicate by chatting in MUDs or while playing online games. MUD stands for Multi-User Dungeon (other types of games call it a MOO, a MUSE, a MUCK, or some other variant; the change in letters simply signifies a different game, and sometimes the letters don't actually stand for anything at all). A MUD is a virtual fantasy word of computer databases where people use words to construct elaborate tales, solve puzzles, battle dragons, stage takeovers and engage in fantasy play. In the right kind of MUD, you (your character) can even kill or die. Chatting while playing online games is also common. In online games, users can pick characters, chat with other users and sometimes even build virtual houses and hold virtual jobs. The popular online game Runescape claims that there are close to 150,000 people playing and chatting online at any one time.[16]

The IRC (Internet Relay Chat) is another method used to chat over the Internet. Using a specific connection number, users can form chat groups on the IRC. Unlike Usenet or a BBS, IRC chat is instantaneous. Users can chat to an entire group or send private messages to each other. IRC is much like a MUD or MOO without the additional fantasy features. However, it is quite common for persons to assume identities that are not their own when chatting using the IRC. In fact, the IRC has been described as "essentially a playground" where persons experiment with different identities and types of self-representation.[17]

Instant messaging allows Internet users to chat with other online users instantaneously by utilizing instant messaging (IM) software. Users of IM software can maintain a list of persons with whom they wish to interact. This list is often called a "buddy list" or "contact list." When a person on a user's buddy list is online, the user is alerted. Most IM software programs provide a variety of features. Using IM software, users can chat with friends online, create custom chat rooms, share a wide variety of file types, and access streaming content that can include real-time stock quotes and news. Popular instant messaging software includes: Yahoo Messenger, AOL Instant Messenger, MSN Messenger and others.

An avenue of Internet communication that is becoming increasingly popular is peer-to-peer (P2P) file-sharing.[18] File-sharing peer-to-peer programs are Internet applications that allow users to download and share files. Peer-to-peer sharing represents a drastic change in the way Internet users traditionally find and exchange information. Users of peer-to-peer file-sharing programs connect to vast numbers of other users and directly share files. This can be done without the intervention of a server, and users can connect directly to the computers of other users.[19] Large groups of users form networks that are extensive, complex and change constantly depending on user activity at any particular moment.

Sharing files using peer-to-peer networks was popularized in the 1990s by the software company Napster. Napster provided free software that allowed users to connect to other users and swap music files. Today users of peer-to-peer networks can swap a wide variety of files, including pornographic videos and pictures.

There are two main types of P2P networks: centralized and decentralized. In a centralized network there is a server or broker that creates a directory of all shared files and directs traffic between users. Often the file names of available files are listed in a large, searchable directory. Napster operated using a centralized model. Because much of the material traded on Napster was copyrighted and Napster brokered the exchange of information, it was vulnerable to legal challenges.[20] Currently, the most popular P2P networks operate using a decentralized model. On these networks users locate other computers and interact directly without a central controller. The Gnutella network was the first popular network to use this model[21] and most newly developed networks are also decentralized.

One unique feature of many peer-to-peer networks is their use of Virtual Name Space (VNS). VNS can associate a user-created name with the Internet address of whatever computer a user happens to connect to a network with. VNS allows point-to-point interaction between individuals and removes the need for users and their computers to know the location and addresses of other users. This feature of peer-to-peer technologies preserves users' anonymity[22] to a certain extent.[23]

Until recently, peer-to-peer networks were associated mainly with downloading music files. This was because Napster only allowed music to be traded. Today, networks like Gnutella allow the trading of many file types. MediaDefender, a company with a specialization in peer-to-peer file-sharing,[24] searched P2P networks and found close to 6,000,000 files they believed were pornographic over a two-day period.[25] MediaDefender claims that pornographic files currently constitute the largest demand for video files on popular P2P networks.

BitTorrent is a peer-to-peer protocol and free, open-source[26] file-sharing program especially for large files. BitTorrent allows users to distribute large files more reliably than common peer-to-peer programs. When a file is published using BitTorrent, every user who wishes to download the file also becomes a distributor. While a user is downloading a file, the bits he or she has already downloaded become available for other users to upload.[27] Thus, unlike most methods of file distribution on the Internet,[28] the more popular a file is, the faster it downloads. This type of file-sharing is growing in popularity, and in 2004 a research firm in the United Kingdom, CacheLogic, estimated that 35% of all Internet traffic was related to BitTorrent.[29] Files commonly distributed using BitTorrent include videos, and software[30] programs. Uses for BitTorrent are still advancing and soon it may be possible to rent videos over the Internet utilizing BitTorrent.[31] In the works are also plans to use a modified BitTorrent client to launch a peer-to-peer television application.[32]

Sexually explicit materials can be transferred through any of the previously mentioned methods that utilize the Internet. I can receive sexually explicit e-mails, visit sites with sexually explicit photos, engage in cyber-sex over chat, download photos or other material from peer-to-peer networks or view pornographic videos downloaded using Bit-Torrent. The possibilities are nearly endless. Furthermore, I can access sexually explicit Internet materials easily over a computer, using many hand-held devices and even over some cellular telephones.

Regulation: Attempts and Possible Regulatory Frameworks

Proponents of Internet regulation raise objections to the fact that there are materials on the Internet that would not be allowed in other media, especially obscenity and pornography. For example, in the United States, obscenity is regulated in all communications technologies. Also, for much pornography in print and film, age is verified before access is allowed. Advocates of regulation claim that the Internet should be regulated in the same fashion that television and radio programs are regulated. Proponents of Internet regulatory methods support their position by arguing that the existence of unregulated obscenity and pornography corrupts minors, harms women and/or contributes to the degradation of morality in society.[33]

Regulation of the sort proposed by proponents of such arguments attempts to restrict materials people receive and/or produce and distribute. All regulatory legislation shares a common goal of preventing undesirable materials from reaching curious eyes and the eyes of those who are involuntarily exposed to such materials. Attempts to regulate Internet materials are common. The United States has sought to protect the curious eyes of children from indecent and obscene materials on the Internet; the European Union and Germany have sought to eliminate materials that contain racism; and France has censored a purloined book. Simultaneously, governments of countries with less-developed telecommunications networks, such as those in Eastern Europe and Asia, have actively promoted limited growth of the Internet

and some Asian countries have sought to control the information dis-
seminated on the Internet so as to align the Internet with the desired
cultural norms in those countries.[34] In this section I will briefly examine attempts at regulation and possible regulatory frameworks.

Examples of proposed and current legislation aimed at regulation
are extensive, as are the methods suggested by which to achieve regulation. One method of regulation frequently suggested would be to hold
Internet Service Providers (ISPs) accountable for material hosted by
their services. This type of regulation may require ISPs to be licensed
much in the same way that radio and television stations are in the United
States. This avenue has been pursued in the case of libel occurring on
the Internet, with conflicting results. In *Cubby, Inc. v. CompuServe*[35]
the ISP, CompuServe,[36] was not held accountable for a defamatory
statement posted on its server. However, in *Stratton Oakmont, Inc. v.
Prodigy Services,*[37] the opposite conclusion was reached and Prodigy,
an ISP, was held accountable for statements on their server. This
method was also used by Germany when it informed the American ISP
CompuServe[38] that it was breaking German obscenity regulations.[39] In
the United States, regulation which involves ISP accountability would
be contradictory to the decision reached in *Smith v. California.* In this
case, it was decided that a bookseller[40] could not reasonably be expected
to know the content of all of the books he or she offers for sale.[41] The
Smith court decided that to impose such a requirement on a bookseller
would be to hinder the free circulation of information. The same problem occurs to an even greater degree on the Internet.

Another possible method of regulation would involve defining a
set or class of material that is to be banned and prosecuting those individuals who make the material available over the Internet. This was
the method chosen by the French government when Dr. Claude Gubler
was prosecuted for uploading a banned book and allowing it to be
downloaded by others on the Internet.[42] In this form of regulation users
would be held accountable for the content they post on the Internet.
In addition, a user may have to obtain a license to post content and
agree not to post banned material.

Australia introduced another regulatory framework for cyber-
speech.[43] This framework applies current classification systems used in

other media to the Internet. Under this classification system, sites would be rated on their violent and sexual content. This is similar to the rating system used for films in the United States. However, in this case, sites receiving a rating indicating a certain level of violent or sexual content would be censored. Breeches of this "broadcasting service amendment" are punishable with fines up to $27,500 per day of violation.[44] To enforce this amendment, Australia has set up a community advisory body called NetAlert.[45]

In response to the availability of sexually explicit Internet materials, the Scottish Parliament is currently considering a proposal to make possession of extreme pornography[46] a crime. Under this proposal, a user who downloads such material could be prosecuted. The maximum penalty for possession of extreme pornography suggested in the proposal is 3 years in prison.[47] This is different from the Australian system as both distributors and consumers of Internet pornography would be subject to prosecution.

In Singapore, both ISPs and Internet users are held accountable for objectionable material. This objectionable material ranges from sexually explicit material to material exposing some political ideas.[48] The government of Singapore has a licensing scheme for all local Internet service providers and content providers designed to eliminate all sexually explicit material.[49] However, some countries have even stricter regulatory laws. In Saudi Arabia and Iran discussions regarding sex (as well as religion and politics) are banned over the Internet.[50] Even more stringent is the Internet censorship sponsored by the government in China.

China openly blocks Internet content and requires Internet cafes to use filtering software that blocks the nearly 500,000 sites banned by the Chinese government.[51] In China there are few Internet access points and all content must pass through government-controlled gateways. By the use of these gateways, the government openly filters sites it believes to contain questionable materials.[52] This type of strict regulation in China can be illustrated in the famous incident involving the popular Internet search engine Google. In September 2002 Chinese governing officials blocked Google in an effort to control the flow of information reaching Chinese citizens.[53] International companies that wish to do business in China are also required to adhere to strict censorship regulation. In December of 2005, Microsoft's MSN network shut down a Chinese blogger's site at the government's request.[54] In a recent article Ben Elgin and Bruce Einhorn outline the enormous efforts the Chinese government expends on Internet censorship. They write, "The agencies that watch over the Net employ over 30,000 people to prowl web sites, blogs, and chat rooms on the lookout for offensive content as well as scammers. In the U.S., by contrast, the entire CIA employs an estimated 16,000 people."[55] Elgin and Einhorn also claim that in China "e-mail with offending words such as 'Taiwan independence' or 'democracy' can be pulled aside and trashed."[56]

In the United States it is unclear what type of regulatory framework legislators envision and who would be held responsible for violations. What is clear, however, is that many legislators believe that some type of regulation is needed. Currently government officials are fighting with the popular search engine Google over the release of records.[57] The records will be used to defend the constitutionality of the Child Online Protection Act (COPA). This attempted defense is the latest in a long history of regulatory attempts.

In 1995 in the United States Senator James Exon, a democrat from Nebraska, introduced the Communications Decency Amendment (CDA). He did this in hopes of preventing the Internet from becoming a red light district and to extend the standards of decency to the Internet. Exon noted that other communications technologies have regulations to protect children that the Internet lacked.[58] The CDA was an attempt to instill such regulations by making it illegal to transmit "indecent" messages over the Internet. The vote in favor of the amendment was 414 to 16 in the House and 91 to 5 in the Senate. Adding the affirmative vote of former president William Clinton, the total tally was 506 out of 527 in favor of the bill.[59] The Supreme Court of the United States did strike down the CDA in *Reno v. The American Civil Liberties Union (ACLU)* in June of 1997.[60] The Court ruled that the CDA would impose a burden on speech that is protected for adults. The next major attempt at regulation in the United States came in the form of the Child Online Protection Act (COPA),[61] which made the transmission of any material "harmful to minors"[62] illegal. Also in December of 2000, the Children's Internet Protection Act was passed. This act forces libraries that receive public funding to utilize blocking software on all computers with Internet access. Besides library use, general efforts to regulate the Internet also continue and many states have Internet regulation laws in existence or currently proposed as lawmakers push forward towards national regulation.

Much of the proposed legislation, at least in the Untied States, relies on placing Internet content into the same category as broadcast speech.[63] The most famous attempt at doing this in the United States was the *Telecommunications Act of 1996.*[64] Despite these attempts, the Internet cannot easily be placed into an already existing category of communication, and many authors have warned against placing Internet speech into previously existing categories. Mike Godwin, representing the Electronic Frontier Foundation, said in a Senate Judiciary Committee hearing that

> the worst mistake we can make on the threshold of this revolution [in Internet communications] is to assume that this new medium is, so far as the Constitution and the laws of the United States are concerned, essentially the same as broadcasting, or more or less similar to telephony. Computer communications — and especially those communications that depend on computer networks of national reach, raise new problems and questions for lawmakers.[65]

Proponents of Internet regulation argue that material on the Internet should not be immune from current regulation. However, making Internet content virtually equivalent to broadcast speech would have broad consequences in the United States. This is mostly due to the precedent set in the case of *FCC v. Pacifica* where the United States Supreme Court ruled that non-obscene material that is "indecent" can be prohibited if non-adults have access to it.[66] Thus, because the Internet is accessible to minors, if Internet content is basically equivalent to broadcast material, "indecent" material can be regulated. However, the Internet is unique and can not be squeezed nicely into the broadcast category.

The Internet Platypus

J. Michael Jaffe compares the Internet to a platypus and writes:

> The platypus is an animal that has the tail of a beaver, a furry body, a duck's bill, and webbed feet. Though classified as a mammal because it nurses its young with milk, its young are hatched from eggs, and biologists are quick to point out complexities of the platypus's attributes in order to appreciate the true nature of the animal. It is only with considerable conceptual effort that the platypus can be categorized within known zoological classes, species, etc.[67]

Jaffe asserts that the Internet, like the platypus, contains many parts of previously classified subjects but is itself hard to classify. This problem of classification and uniqueness makes creating a regulatory framework appropriate for the Internet difficult, if not impossible.

In the United States, different forms of communicative technology are given different degrees of First Amendment protection because of the individual characteristics of each medium. Justification for the regulatory power given to the Federal Communications Commission (FCC) has, generally, been based on two characteristics of broadcasting. One of these is that broadcasting is "uniquely pervasive" and tends to have a captive audience.[68] The other characteristic is that the number of available broadcasting frequencies are limited.[69] To the extent that these two criteria are applicable to a medium, regulations allowed by the Court have varied.[70]

For example in the aforementioned case of *Pacifica Foundation v. FCC* the Court justified a ban on the radio station broadcast of comedian George Carlin due to the fact that radio invades the home and is easily accessible by children.[71] The restrictions on radio also apply to broadcast television. The FCC is free to control the content aired on broadcast television and make restrictions on time of day and types of material allowed in the United States.

Cable television also can have a pervasive presence in a viewer's home (if it is purchased) but does not suffer from scarcity of frequency. Given this, it is not surprising that the Court has affirmed fewer regulations on cable television than on radio and public television. An example of this is found in *Denver Area Educational Telecommunications Consortium, Inc. v. FCC* where the Court struck down two provisions of the 1992 Cable Act that promoted heavy regulations.[72] Despite such rulings, regulation advocates often focus on cable television. In Utah, anti-indecency laws that criminalize distribution of indecency by "wire or cable" have been passed and invalidated many times.[73]

For telephonic communication, the Court did not uphold a ban on the transmission of indecent speech (dial-a-porn or commercial phone sex) because, unlike radio, the Court concluded that a caller must take affirmative steps[74] to access such material and there is less chance that such material will be accessed accidentally. This decision is represented in *Sable Communication, Inc. v. FCC*. While the Court did recognize the need to protect children in this case it found that, because of the nature of telephonic communications, there were less restrictive ways to do so than a ban on all indecent speech over the telephone.

The Internet is clearly different from any of these aforementioned communications technologies. Like dial-a-porn users, the computer user must take deliberate steps to invite the Internet into his or her home. These steps include subscribing to an ISP, choosing to continue that subscription, buying and configuring a computer or Internet-enabled device, dialing into the service and using the Internet.[75] The Internet also does not suffer from scarcity of frequency. On the contrary, whenever a new computer connects to the Internet the overall capacity increases. On the other hand, cyber-speech is also quite different from printed speech. These differences include the ease with which it is accessed,[76] as well as the possible multimedia dimensions beyond those of traditional communications mediums.[77]

The Internet blurs the distinction between content producers and content consumers. This is because everyone on the Internet can produce and consume content with relative ease. As Howard Rheingold writes, "[W]ith the right knowledge, and not too much of it, a ten-year-old kid can plug these two vast, powerful, expensively developed technologies[78] together for a few hundred dollars and instantly obtain a bully pulpit, the Library of Congress, and a world full of potential coconspirators."[79] There is no coherent homology between cyberspace and real space as there is no reliable way to map the physical location of an information consumer or information distributor. Even if an Internet address can tell us something about the location of a machine that stores information it tells us nothing about the physical location of the machine's operator. In fact, an operator may have accounts on computers all over the world and use an Internet application called Telnet to effortlessly access each account.

Most newspapers are local devices and radio and television are often geographically contained by the strength of a signal. However, the Internet is not geographically located in any one spot. In fact, it is often impossible to decipher the origin of Internet content that has been passed thorough a remailer and encrypted using one of the widely available public key encryption tools. Neither the information provider nor the information consumer can reliably be physically located. This makes online commerce doubly blind. Thus, it is more difficult, if not impossible, to trace the source of some material for the purpose of regulation.

The Internet is truly a unique medium. In a sense, it is a combination of all previous communications methods with some truly novel elements included. While there are clear differences between broadcast speech and cyber-speech, it is often argued that these differences make it *more* imperative that steps at regulation be taken. However, it is unlikely that any preexisting regulatory framework can be applied to the Internet. In the next chapter I will examine one such attempt to apply a framework in the case of the regulation of Internet obscenity.

2

The Failure of Current Legislation: Obscenity and Community Standards in the United States

Introduction

Recently the United States Supreme Court decided to uphold the injunction against the Child Online Protection Act (COPA), which was signed into law on October 21, 1998.[1] One of the concerns presented by the Court was that a community standards based regulatory approach might not be appropriate for the Internet.[2] However, such a standard is currently used for regulating Internet obscenity in the United States and, despite the common conception, the Internet is not a haven for free speech. While it was decided in the United States in *Stanley v. Georgia*[3] that possessing obscene material, except child pornography, in a person's own home is protected by the First Amendment, it is illegal to post or transfer obscene material on the Internet. Regulation of such obscenity on the Internet is based on the current obscenity standard defined in *Miller v. California*.[4] If this regulatory system were justified and effective for Internet material, it would be pointless to continue this chapter; however, there are serious questions concerning the use of a community standards based approach in the regulation of Internet content. Problems that many authors have associated with current obscenity regulation[5] are magnified on the Internet. These obstacles, ubiquitous in the current obscenity standard, make it hopeless to apply such regulation justly to Internet content. In this chapter, I will offer a brief overview of obscenity regulation and argue that current standards (and perhaps any standards) are unsuitable for the regulation of Internet obscenity.

The Current Standard: An Obscene History

Before the Civil War there were few obscenity prosecutions in the United States.[6] However, this situation was significantly altered after the war by Anthony Comstock, who vigorously campaigned to prohibit obscenity and increase the number of obscenity prosecutions. Comstock's concerns seemed to be centered on the protection of children from pornographic materials and moral decline in society. In his book, *Traps for the Young*, written in 1883, Comstock asserted that pornography was a trap for innocent youth set by Satan.[7] Comstock was especially concerned that falling into this "trap" would cause previously innocent children to practice self-abuse.[8] Of such self-abuse Comstock writes:

> Is not this awful curse to the young prevalent enough to command a remedy? To call for attention from parents? Go to the insane asylums and epileptic hospitals for a reply. Our youth are falling on every side. Lives that otherwise might shine as the stars in the firmament are shrouded with a veil of darkness, with horrors to the victim's mind which no pen can describe.[9]

As a result of Comstock's efforts, the United States Congress passed the Comstock Act in 1873, which prohibited the mailing of obscene[10] material.[11] After this new interest in obscenity emerged, the struggle to define what exactly constituted obscenity started in the United States. This search for a definition led to the current obscenity standard in the United States.

The standard's early roots can be traced back to the British case of *Regina v. Hicklin*.[12] In this case, decided in 1868, Lord Chief Justice Cockborn concluded that the publication in question, *The Confessional*

Unmasked: Shewing the Depravity of the Romanish Priesthood, the Iniquity of the Confessional and the Questions Put to Females in Confession, was obscene. Cockborn based his decision on his belief that the work "would suggest to the minds of the young of either sex, or even to persons of more advanced years, thoughts of a most impure and libidinous character."[13] Cockborn, was especially concerned that these thoughts would be corrupting to morals and held that the proper test for obscenity was "whether the tendency of the matter charged as obscenity is to deprave and corrupt those whose minds are open to such immoral influences[14] and into whose hands a publication of this sort may fall."[15] The standard developed in cases such as *Roth v. United States, Alberts v. California,*[16] and *Memoirs v. Massachusetts,*[17] however, it received refinement in *Miller v. California.* In *Miller v. California,* the current three-prong test for obscenity was developed. The three-prong test outlined in the Court's opinion is the following: (1) whether "the average person, applying contemporary community standards" would find that the work, taken as a whole, appeals to the prurient[18] interest; (2) whether the work depicts or describes, in a patently offensive[19] way, sexual conduct specifically defined by the applicable state law; and (3) whether the work, taken as a whole, lacks serious[20] literary, artistic, political, or scientific value.[21] Thus, if a picture, text, performance or sound satisfies all three prongs of the test, it is legally obscene.

The idea that existing standards[22] used for regulating communication technologies should be applied to the Internet is common. For example, in defense of the Broadcasting Service Amendment of 1999, Australian Senator Richard Alston claims,

> The existing classification system for film, television, and other media was established to provide guidance to the community, and particularly to concerned parents, on the suitability or otherwise of content. Based on contemporary community standards, this system is well understood and accepted within our society. Given the legitimate and increasing community concerns about the offensive nature of some online material and the easy accessibility of that material, the Government considered it a logical step to legislate to extend the classification system to the Internet.[23]

Alston further claims that a "do nothing" approach would mean that current community standards should not apply to the Internet. Despite

Alston's optimism, there are vast difficulties with applying the current obscenity standard in the United States to Internet content. One such problem is the lack of a coherent definition as to what is or is not obscene.

Problems with Miller

In cases decided after *Miller,* the United States Supreme Court has assumed that obscenity exists and defined it in accordance with *Miller.* Thus, the Court defines obscenity by terms such as "patent offensiveness" and "prurient interests."[24] Despite its extensive history, I believe this definition is so vague that it does not allow a distributor of potentially obscene materials to receive fair warning. For example: "offensive," "prurient interest" and "serious value" can all be interpreted in many different ways by different persons. What one person finds offensive another may not. Also, what excites one person sexually (creates a prurient interest) may not excite another and what one person considers to be of serious value another may not. Given this vagueness, such a definition will be ineffectual in providing guidance for regulation. In order to know what to regulate and provide fair warning to those who publish what could be considered objectionable materials, it is necessary for a better definition of obscenity to be formulated. However, a satisfactory definition has yet to be provided. William Linsley writes: "the line that separates the obscene, the pornographic, the licentious, the lewd, the libidinous, the prurient, the lascivious, the indecent, the smutty, and the filthy from each other is imperceptible."[25] Given this vagueness, there exist no clear legal standards regarding illicit expression because the law itself cannot define terms like *obscenity* or even terms like *depraved, corrupt, indecent* or *disgusting*, which are often added in an effort to better pin down what obscenity means. Thus, we are left with Supreme Court justices such as Potter Stewart who, although he admitted that he could not define what obscenity is, said, "I know it when I see it."[26] Even Supreme Court Justice Brennan, who advocated the formulation of current obscenity law for many years, has concluded that providing a clear definition of obscenity may be impossible. Brennan once lamented to a reporter about his ability to define obscenity. He said, "I tried and tried, and I waffled back and forth, and I finally gave up. If you can't define it, you can't prosecute people for it."[27]

A further complication is that it is impossible to determine by content alone what is obscene. This is, in part, due to different standards across time and jurisdiction. Obscenity is a legal term, not a moral one. It, in and of itself, does not describe any characteristic or group of characteristics contained in any object. To be obscene, as the law defines such a status, is to belong to a legal class of things, which varies over time and place. This is because attitudes and views about what is appropriate and offensive change over time in communities.[28] As Harry White writes, "one reason we cannot arrive at a consistent definition or a universal standard of obscenity is that the term does not define an objective characteristic of a work but various subjective responses to it."[29] The statement "object A is obscene" lacks verifiability. Unlike the statement "snow is white," we cannot show that something is obscene by appealing to empirical evidence alone. In fact, no evidence about object A itself can show that it is obscene. Therefore the statement, "object A is obscene," cannot be true or false without further information. While it can be true or false to say that object A is considered obscene in place B at time C, this imparts little information about object A itself and more about responses to object A. This leaves open the possibility that what is obscene to one person may not be to another. While it is true that in many instances all conditions for truth need not be within the object itself,[30] this creates complications for a potential distributor of material that is potentially obscene. The main complication is simply in ascertaining when something is obscene and when it is not.

This complication, in and of itself, may not be a hindrance for regulation. Given that the sentence "object A is obscene at place B at time C" can be verified, it is possible that regulation could be based on what is obscene in certain communities at certain times. This is precisely what a community standards based approach, like that set out in *Miller v. California,* would ideally accomplish. However, while such standards may (or may not) be workable in a physical community limited by geographic boundaries, they certainly are problematic when stretched to apply to the Internet.

The question of what constitutes a community is nebulous even when geographical borders help define the community. In *Hamling v. United States*[31] the United States Supreme Court analyzed the breadth of a relevant community. In this case the court stated that the standards of a community were not to be thought of as a "hypothetical and unascertainable national standard." In *Miller v. California*, the state of California was considered a community.[32] However in *Hamling*, the court emphasized that the geographic boundary used in *Miller* was not mandated.[33] Thus, areas both smaller and larger than a state could be a community for regulatory purposes in the United States. This makes the legal standard as to what constitutes a community somewhat nebulous. Given this, where community standards[34] are to originate is equally troublesome.

While uncertainly surrounds the Court's aforementioned decisions, what is clear is that geographical location plays an important part in determining the boundaries of a community. However, material on the Internet does not have a set geographical location. In fact, the nature of the Internet makes governance by geographical boundaries practically impossible.

Community Standards for the Internet?

Even if we could pin down what a community consists of, the question remains as to what would be an appropriate community standard to guide obscenity regulation of Internet materials. There are three possible relevant communities that could be considered when applying community standards to Internet content. The relevant community could be the community in which a viewer downloads the material. Another approach could be to hold the relevant community standard to be that from which the material originates. The third possibility would be to appeal to virtual communities and to hold the Internet itself (or parts of it) as an independent community or communities.

In the legal case involving Robert and Carleen Thomas, the community of the viewer was assumed[35] to be the proper community to use in the regulation of obscenity. The Thomases operated an electronic bulletin board system from their California home. Their board was called "All Amateur Action" and catered to adults by offering sexually explicit photographs and descriptions. Only members, who paid a monthly fee for entrance, were permitted to access the photographs. The Thomases took great care to ensure that their members were adults.[36] While the bulletin board refused to offer child pornography, it did offer photographs that were quite explicit.[37] It was photographs of this sort that caught the eye[38] of postal inspector David Dirmeyer from Memphis. After investigating the board by becoming a member and downloading many photographs, Dirmeyer asserted that the Thomases were selling and transmitting material that was obscene by Memphis community standards.[39] The computers used for the bulletin board were seized and the Thomases were charged with knowingly using and causing to be used a means of interstate commerce for the purpose of transporting obscene, computer-generated materials in interstate commerce.[40] The Thomases, who were sentenced in Tennessee, attempted to have their case moved to California. However, the district court judge denied their pre-trial motions. The judge concluded that the trial should take place in Tennessee because it was Memphis that was affected by the distribution of the allegedly obscene material. This trial resulted in a conviction and prison terms[41] for both Carleen and Robert.[42] The Thomases appealed to the Sixth Circuit Court of Appeals and faced another unfavorable decision.[43] The Thomas family did not know they were committing a crime, and believed their material was legal because they purchased it from pornography stores in San Francisco.[44] In fact, two years prior to their indictment in Tennessee, law-enforcement officials in San Jose, California, investigated the Thomases and determined that the material on the board did not violate the community standards of San Jose.[45]

Given the current standard, the court made what was, perhaps, a reasonable decision in the case.[46] The court decided to uphold the conviction because, according to the current standard, it would appear that the community standards of Memphis were violated. In addition, because Robert and Carleen knew the information on their BBS was sent to Memphis, the court concluded that their conviction was not significantly different than traditional obscenity cases in which materials are sent by postal mail.[47]

However, the Thomas case shows the difficulty and chilling effect on speech that using the community of the viewer as the proper community standard by which to judge obscenity would entail. Usually in the United States, to be convicted of a crime, one must have known that he or she was committing a crime or be blatantly negligent in allowing a crime to occur. While Robert and Carleen required knowledge of the physical location of their users, most content providers do not. These providers, given that material posted on the Internet can reach a global audience, would have to be superhuman to be able to judge if the material were deemed obscene by any community in which their material can be accessed.[48]

A provider of Internet content, even one such as the Thomases, should not be reasonably expected to have knowledge of the community standards in every community, perhaps every city, where members reside. Even juries consisting of members of a given community have difficulty determining what constitutes the proper community standard by which to judge obscenity. Jurors, even if instructions are given, typically decide obscenity cases using their personal morals and judgments.[49] In many ways, even a member of a given community will not be able to ascertain the community's general standards concerning obscenity. I do not know what will constitute obscenity to my neighbor and certainly am unable to speak for the entire community, assuming I have any idea of where to draw a community boundary. This is due partially to the fact that communities are made up of diverse populations. In addition, I have not had contact with a majority of the persons residing in my community and, thus, cannot speak for them. These concerns are greatly magnified when the global nature of the Internet is considered. As David Loundy writes about the Thomases' case, "[I]nstead of Agent Dirmeyer, an inspector could just as easily have been calling from one of the countries in, for example, the Middle East where women run the risk of being stoned to death or spat upon for not wearing a veil in public." This is a similar situation to the one that CompuServe faced in 1995 as it banned access to nearly 200 discussion groups to avoid being prosecuted under German obscenity laws.[50]

In real space a business can usually locate the geographical location of the persons it is interacting with; however, this is not always possible in cyberspace. While some online distributors may require a billing address,[51] many accept online payment services or are free to consumers.[52] Screening or blocking Internet resources by country or state is also very difficult, if not impossible. Internet protocols were not designed to facilitate geographic documentation; in fact, they ignore it. While URLs act as addresses of some sort, they locate a machine's position on the network, not in real space. While some Internet addresses do contain a geographic locator, like the domain ".uk," most do not. Also, a user could be using an account or address that has nothing to do with his or her physical location. A user can remotely log in and even anonymously log in to an account across the country or across the world and use it to access information. Combined with features such as remote access and anonymous login, there are few, if any, clues left that would allow a content provider to screen users by geographic location. This is not to mention the many ways that users could actively conceal their location and identity.[53] Also, the packets of information themselves may travel along many routes which the content provider does not control. When information is requested from one computer to another on the Internet, depending on local traffic, a remote route may be faster for the information to travel on. Therefore, technically, a distributor cannot possibly know where he or she is "distributing" his or her packets of information. This is even more complicated when using a program like BitTorrent. Those that download files using BitTorrent also become distributors to a multitude of unknown users.

Of course, a potential distributor could limit distribution to the community standard of the most morally rigid community to eliminate the risk of a conviction. To do this, however, would be to dramatically limit speech. Unlike print media, a distributor of sexually explicit material cannot chose not to mail his or her materials to only certain communities. In many societies in which Internet materials could be accessible, representations of persons in underwear and even pictures of the unveiled face of some women could be considered obscene. Even in the United States, in cities such as Cincinnati, Ohio, some depictions have been judged to be obscene that are not considered obscene in other communities. Such was the case when the director of the Cincinnati Museum of Art, Dennis Barrie, was arrested for exhibiting the homo-erotic photographs of a well-recognized artist, Robert Mapplethorpe.[54] To err on the safe side would reduce the Internet to the lowest common denominator and silence work that may be of great social value but which, in some community somewhere, may be considered obscene. In addition, some particularly motivated prosecutors could easily abuse this standard and shop for the most conservative community in which to claim that obscenity standards have been violated.[55]

Given all these problems, using the community of the viewer as a relevant community standard is not acceptable. Given this, I will examine another possible solution: using the community in which the material originates as the relevant community by which to judge obscenity. While this solution would alleviate any concern of prosecutors "shopping" for conservative communities, it is not unproblematic.

With the previous possible community standard the most conservative community could set the standard for the Internet; however, with this solution, the opposite problem may appear. Instead of the most conservative community, the most permissive one could be used to set the community standards for the entire Internet. This is because persons who transmit material in one community can easily transfer their accounts, and thus base of operations, in a matter of minutes. Thereby they would gain shelter from a permissive community. This is accomplished with ease because all Internet addresses are inherently portable. Today the materials distributed on the porn.com domain may originate from a computer operating in New Zealand. However, tomorrow the owner of the domain may transfer his operation to a host machine in London. The operator would not be required to move to the location of the host machine where his information originates. In fact, with a few clicks of his mouse, he can set up operations almost anywhere. This transfer would be completely invisible to his customers. Thus, if the community in which the material originates were used as the relevant community a cyber-version of Sodom and Gomorrah[56] could set the community standards for the Internet.[57] This would be especially troublesome if a country that allowed clearly abhorrent materials, like child pornography, were allowed to set the standard.

Also, the question of where exactly the material originates is difficult given the nature of the Internet. Unlike materials carried by traditional methods, it is often impossible to know where Internet content comes from. Remailers combined with public key encryption allow virtually anonymous communication. Thus, if one cannot determine the community from which the material originates, it would be impossible to use such a community as a relevant community standard.

A third possible community standard would treat "virtual communities" or cyberspace itself as the relevant community by which to regulate sexually explicit materials. The nature of the Internet, which allows for connections between multiple parties in many geographic locales, makes this solution plausible. Dawn Kaplan and others have suggested that a "community of cyberspace" be used as a relevant community standard.[58] Such a solution would alleviate many concerns expressed concerning the previous possible community standards and allow those who are affected by Internet materials to determine a relevant standard.

To treat cyberspace itself as a community is clearly not feasible as the variety of persons accessing the Internet is almost as great as those living in physical space. If a jury could be drawn from all Internet users, they would clearly be diverse and find it impossible to draw a common standard. This would bring us back to square one. Thus, we are left with the possibility of using virtual communities.

Without geographic boundaries, the idea of a "virtual community" seems awkward. However, there are plausible communities currently intact that do not have geographic boundaries. Through membership in the American Philosophical Association and conference attendance, I sense that I am part of the philosophical community (especially the small part of it consisting of philosophers who share similar interests to my own). I have forged this association by networking and forming relationships among other members of this community. Often at conferences we have talked face-to-face but other times, we have merely been privileged to read publications or e-mail comments on our works in progress to one another. Members of this community help one another (for the most part) and share both the glory of success and disappointments. Of course, I do not interact with every member of the community just as the members of a physical community do not befriend every other member. Some members I know only by their writings or have merely witnessed presenting their work.

Another example of a community that is not dependent on a physical location is that of the "Deadheads."[59] The Deadheads are a group of persons who used to follow the musical band the Grateful Dead. The Deadheads would travel in microbuses and set up camp wherever the Grateful Dead happened to be playing. While the Deadheads lack a defined physical location they have many features of a community. The Deadheads have their own culture, which includes heavy use of recreational drugs and common use of terms and phrases which are meaningless to someone outside their culture. The Deadheads also have a sense of common purpose and shared adversity. This shared adversity is most commonly directed at the Drug Enforcement Administration. In many ways the Deadheads have a community.

Of course, such communities are quite different from what Gordon Graham, author of *The Internet: A Philosophical Inquiry*, lists as a paradigm community: a contained religious community.[60] Examples of such religious communities are convents and monasteries. In such communities the members are bound together through the common law of the religious community and the religion itself. Also, the members are usually geographically bound and live a truly communal lifestyle. However, if all communities were expected to cohere closely to a paradigmatic example, we would be left with very few communities. Also, it seems very plausible that a community of Deadheads who share a common cause (like a religious community) is closer to the paradigm than most current geographical communities.

While certainly not all voluntary associations of individuals are communities, it is reasonable to claim that some are, even some whose members do not share a geographical proximity. Thus, geographical proximity may not be a necessary ingredient in the definition of a community. To help define (I am doubtful that a full definition can ever be given) a community apart from geographical boundaries it is helpful to use the conception of an experiential community.[61] What the essential features of such a community consist of has been the subject of many works. The most commonly cited and coherent necessary characteristics that define a community are: shared experiences, a feeling of belonging, personal investment among members, established boundaries, the ability to distinguish members from non-members, some group control over governance and sustained interaction among members.[62] I believe these criteria offer at least the beginning of a definition of community, as it would be dubious for associations among persons to be labeled a community that lacked any one of the aforementioned characteristics.

Agora describes a historical meeting place that was usually located in the center of a city. In such a place, merchants would bring their wares to sell and citizens would exchange ideas. In other words, it was a community gathering place. Perhaps the Internet can provide such gathering places. While there is reason to be skeptical about the existence of virtual communities,[63] there is compelling evidence that some may exist. The WELL (Whole Earth Electronic Link) and Lambda-MOO are two often-cited examples of such communities. The WELL is a large conferencing system whose members have contributed greatly to the literature on virtual communities. LambdaMOO, however, is known for an incident where a group member transgressed unwritten norms in the community and was subject to punishment.

In most cases, members of an Internet "community" believe they can recognize where the boundaries of a virtual community are and, in many cases, visitors and members of the community are required to enter a user name and password or perform a special action to enter the community. Once inside, the range of actives and interactions occurring in the virtual community is vast. In his book, *The Virtual Community*, Howard Rheingold gives a detailed account of being a member of the WELL. Of the WELL and other virtual communities Reingold writes:

> People in virtual communities use words on screens to exchange pleasantries and argue, engage in intellectual discourse, conduct commerce, exchange knowledge, share emotional support, make plans, brainstorm, gossip, feud, fall in love, find friends and lose them, play games, flirt, create a little high art and a lot of idle talk. People in virtual communities do just about everything people do in real life, but we leave our bodies behind. You can't kiss anybody and nobody can punch you in the nose, but a lot can happen within those boundaries.[64]

This clearly suggests that there are shared experiences among WELL members.

Rheingold believes that the WELL qualifies as a community and personally senses a feeling of community while participating in the WELL. Of the other members of the WELL Rheingold claims, "I care about these people I met through my computer"[65] and "I have good friends now all over the world who I never would have met without the mediation of the Internet."[66] These inhabitants of virtual communities are often referred to as *netizens*. Rheingold describes the WELL as "a small town"[67] and claims that netizens support one another and often lend a virtual hand to other community members. A particularly vivid examples of this is when Rheingold writes about his experience participating in an emotional support group for a WELL friend whose son had recently been diagnosed with leukemia.[68] Another commentator, Mike Godwin, has also written of his experience with the WELL. Godwin claims, "if that neighborly sense of belonging doesn't prove the existence of a community, I don't know what does."[69]

Now that it is clear that at least some virtual communities have defined boundaries and that that their members share experiences and have a feeling of community, it is important to examine the other necessary characteristics of communities. The time spent getting to know other netizens and providing support to them certainly qualifies as a personal investment for members of virtual communities. Perhaps due to this time invested, members can usually spot a visitor or new netizen quite easily. When a new user enters a virtual community the regulars exhibit a blend of curiosity and cautiousness. Instead of bringing cookies or other baked goods to a new neighbor, it has been my experience that netizens tend to bring cautious enthusiasm and advice. Often more established members of virtual communities offer to help a new user navigate the community or learn commands. When I entered Lambda-MOO for the first time I was greeted by several regular participants who offered to help if I found myself stuck in the any of the "rooms." It was certainly obvious that I was recognized as an outsider.

Governance of virtual communities varies greatly. It can consist merely of unwritten norms, guidelines given and regulations placed on conduct by systems operators (sysops) or more extensive, formally enforced rules. Quite often sysops banish members of a virtual community or members ban together to decide that an unruly member must be ousted.[70] Many authors have discussed how members of both LambdaMOO and the WELL have ousted members after group discussion.[71] In fact, the event that made LambdaMOO famous (or perhaps infamous) involved members of the virtual community reprimanding a member for improper behavior.

In LambdaMOO, a member, Mr. Bungle, used a Voodoo doll program[72] to virtually "rape" other members of the MOO. This was accomplished by using the Voodoo doll program to attribute behaviors and words to other characters against the will of the actor playing the character. In particular, Mr. Bungle used the program to make other characters appear to engage in violent sexual relations with his character. While I am dubious that using such a program to virtually force characters to engage in online sexual relations constitutes rape, it is clear that this action by Mr. Bungle violated the norms of the MOO. In response to this violation, the members of LambdaMOO came together and initiated a disciplinary measure. The users of LambdaMOO decided to banish Mr. Bungle from the MOO.[73] Given this story and others like it, it is evident that in at least some virtual communities there is group governance by members. Thus, it appears as if all the listed necessary conditions for being a community can be met by some virtual communities. Given this, it is possible to seriously consider using virtual communities to be the relevant community standard by which to judge obscenity. However, there are some key differences between physical and virtual communities.

One difference between virtual and real communities is that members in virtual communities can remain anonymous and often are not who they make themselves out to be. Consider again the case of LambdaMOO. LambdaMOO, which has been written about as a "community," seems far from one. In fact, it is hard to think of MUDs and MOOs as anything more than elaborate games. Rheingold writes of MUDs, "magic is real and identity is fluid."[74] In MUDs people pretend to be someone else, several other people or assume an entirely different identity such as an animal or inanimate object like a toaster. One of the victims of the "rape" in LambdaMOO was Legba, a "Haitian

41

trickster sprit of indeterminate gender."[75] Also involved in the event was "Bakunin" (the well-known radical), and Juniper (the squirrel).[76] Unless squirrels have developed the ability and desire to participate in MOOs, and Haitian trickster sprits roam the world, it is clear that the persons using LambdaMOO are not who they claim to be. Lambda-MOO is not alone and many virtual "communities" encourage identity fabrication.

Even in communities where characters are not as outrageous as LambdaMOO, there is still quite a bit of deception. There is a well-publicized case that illustrates such deception involving CompuServe and "Joan." The case occurred in 1995, early in the history of virtual community building. Joan presented herself as a neuropsychologist who had been involved in an accident that left her disabled, crippled and mute. Joan was readily accepted on CompuServe and many women credit her as helping them through problems and being an intimate and close friend. However, in reality, Joan was a psychiatrist who did not have a disability and was male. This psychiatrist, Alex, was simply experimenting with being a trusted female virtual companion.[77] Once the deception was revealed, many of "Joan's" friends tried to befriend Alex but found that they were not compatible.[78] While members of Compu-Serve felt deceived, such character building and identity fabrication is now the norm over the Internet.[79] For some persons participating in virtual communities is merely a game.

Given this ambiguity, it is quite possible that imaginary characters cannot sustain a meaningful community. Although the characters may interact with one another, it is not evident that they are real interactions. Perhaps a type of physical interaction is necessary for a community. Consider the physical aspects of the WELL. While the WELL contains members from many countries, it is centered in the San Francisco Bay area and members often physically interact. Of this geographic center Rheingold writes, "the WELL felt like an authentic community from the start because it was grounded in my everyday physical world."[80] Perhaps some type of physical interaction (or possibility of such interaction) is necessary in a community.

Anonymity may also encourage outrageous behavior because there is not an opportunity for recourse. It is a type of Gyges Ring[81] and can be illustrated by the fact that most harassing notes are anonymous. While this is not specific to the Internet, it is quite possible that, given the great degree of anonymity available, it is magnified. As Plato was aware, people are simply more likely to do outrageous and/or immoral things when their identity is shielded. Perhaps because of this level of anonymity, even Rheingold admits that some newsgroups are "more like battlefields than communities."[82]

Rheingold tries to lessen this difference between real and virtual communities when he writes, "You can be fooled by people in cyber-space, behind the cloak of words. But that can also be said about telephones or face-to-face communication."[83] While his response is true to some degree, it is also true that in real communities it is much harder to fool those around you. Recently I moved into a small town (one in which the welcome wagon still functions and stoplights are unnecessary) and realized just how nosey neighbors can be. After the initial gifts of cookies and strudel[84] the questions started. In addition, the neighbors kept a careful eye on my possessions being carried into the house and soon started arriving at the front door to "welcome" my family. There are some things that I simply cannot, at least without great effort, fool my neighbors about. If I were to tell them that I was a short, balding man they would not believe me.[85] In addition, they know when I leave the house, when I turn my lights on at night and even when I walk my dog. While I may be able to sustain certain types of lies, there are many that would quickly be unmasked. In order to gain employment, rent an apartment, or even open a checking account certain information is checked. This information usually includes identity (including gender and date of birth), police records and credit records. Thus, if I wish to involve myself in the community by becoming employed or establishing a residence, certain information about me will have already been revealed.

While this intrusiveness can be annoying, it is not without reason. My neighbors must decide what kind of a person I am for several reasons. Perhaps they wish to leave their children home alone for a brief period or want to leave their home unlocked. To do either of these things, they must have reason to suspect that I am not a kleptomaniac or child murderer. While I may be able to fool them about who I am, it is much more difficult than in a virtual community. Neighbors in real communities rely on one another, join common causes and even trust one another with their children and property. This trust would be hard to replicate in a virtual community due to the ease of deception.

Another stark difference between virtual and real communities is that citizens have a deep and multifaceted personal investment in a real community. In a sense, a community may help define a citizen's identity and be a part of who he or she is. This investment is financial, familial and personal. In my recent move I had a chance to witness just how invested I was in my community. As I said goodbye to my family members, moved checking accounts, changed driver's licenses, bought new insurance, signed my child into his new school and struggled to find my way around, I realized how invested I was in my former community. In a virtual community the process of moving is quite a bit easier. There are no personal belonging to pile into a U-Haul while making sure that your grandmother's mirror is not broken. All a person has to do is log into another community. Of course, there may be a "getting to know you" period for him or her (or his or her character) in the new community and even some emotional investment, but this ignores all other levels of investment. Members of virtual communities do not have to worry if their children will hate them for pulling them away from their old friends or if they will be secure financially in the new location: they simply leave.

Given the aforementioned differences it is reasonable to be leery about considering virtual communities to be real communities. In addition, even if they were real communities, using them as a community standard may still be unworkable. One of the problems with using a virtual community standard is that, like real communities, virtual communities are incredibly diverse. Of virtual communities David Loundy writes, "[P]ictures showing people having sex with horses may offend local standards in a 'community' such as Prodigy (which prides itself in having a 'family' atmosphere), or in Tennessee, but may not offend the standards in California or on parts of the Internet."[86] Given this, it would have to be decided if the relevant virtual community standard was the virtual community which received the potential obscenity or that from which it originated. The problems with using either of these alternatives would parallel those involved in using physical communities. If the virtual community that received the information were chosen, the Internet would likely have to conform to the most conservative virtual community.[87] However, if the originating community were chosen, the most permissive community could set the standard, thereby making obscenity regulation nonsensical.

Due to the failure of a plausible community standard to be drawn, I offer a fourth possibility. This possibility is to admit that community standards cannot be used for Internet regulation. The entire existence of Internet materials simply occurs outside of our current notions of geographically bound community. Physical locality makes little sense on a global information network and I am dubious that the notion of a virtual community can help save the community standards based legislation.

An Alternative and Objections

Even if a community standards approach fails to provide a means for disallowing material to be on the Internet, there is another potential arena for obscenity regulation: a community could decide that they simply do not want Internet obscenity in their community. While this may, at first glance, seem to be a horrible invasion, there are many similar existing laws. There are laws in many communities that dictate if one can build a shed on one's property, play loud music, park in certain areas, walk naked down the street or even drive a certain speed. Last year I received fines for committing two similar offenses (letting my cat outside and parking with a wheel of my car on my grass). While there may be nothing objectively wrong with building a shed or letting a cat outside, the community members have decided that not doing these things would make the community a better place in which to live. The same may be true of accessing obscenity in certain communities.

An immediate objection to regulation of this sort could be made in that the laws previously mentioned are in place due to the possible effects of one community member's action on another community member. From this, it is reasonable to conclude that regulating obscenity that is viewed in the privacy of one's own home is very much unlike the previously mentioned laws because it may only initially affect the willing viewer.[88] While this objection is reasonable it is also the case that many laws are in place that do regulate what persons do in the privacy of their homes. Examples include laws regulating sodomy. Of course the descriptive fact that such laws are in place does not lead to the normative conclusion that they should be in place. However, it does point to the fact that, in the United States, communities may have the authority to make such laws. Even if such laws should not be in place, a proponent of community regulation of Internet obscenity could side-step the issue and simply argue that community members should not be allowed to view obscenity in public places. This is similar to arguments given in regard to viewing pornography in public libraries. Therefore, this objection need not be fatal to proponents of community regulation of Internet obscenity.

Another objection to community regulation of Internet obscenity could invoke the previously mentioned problems in defining what is obscene. Given the vagueness involved in the obscenity definition, it could be argued that community regulation is impossible due to the fact that community members will not agree on what is obscene. However, the fact that members of a community may not all agree on what should be considered obscene need not be an important factor when considering regulation of this type. This is clear when considering examples such as speed limits. For any given street there is bound to be some disagreement about what a "proper" speed limit would be. Furthermore, there is quite a bit of gray area around what is a safe speed on the road. Some community members may favor a higher speed than others; however, coming to a consensus is not only reasonable but also necessary to avoid accidents. The same could be the case in the regulation of Internet obscenity; although there may be some differences of opinion, a consensus may be reached. However, this is not the case.

The subjectivity involved in defining what is or is not obscene is much different than that of assigning a speed limit. After the initial consensus is agreed upon to set a speed limit, Citizen Jones, even if he did not agree with the consensus, is bound by the limit set. Jones knows that if he drives over the speed limit he is subject to a speeding ticket.

All Jones needs to do is look at his speedometer to know if he is acting lawfully. In this case, Jones is clearly warned what the consequences of his actions are and knows how to avoid breaking the law. However, a case involving Citizen Smith who views Internet content is quite different. The community in which Citizen Smith lives could decide that obscene material cannot, by force of law, be viewed on the Internet. Smith knows that if he views such material, he will be subject to punishment. However, Smith would soon encounter difficulties. Smith may wish to view the Victoria's Secret catalogue online, visit a virtual exhibit of the work of photographer Robert Mapplethorpe or look at the scans from a philatelist who has stamps featuring Goya's nudes. Any one of these activities could be obscene to different members of Smith's community. While community members could join together and try to develop criteria to be used in making judgments, this is unlikely to be an adequate solution. Given the failure of attempts to establish criteria or define obscenity in the past, it will be unlikely that newly formulated criteria will be reasonable and able to address the wide variety of material available. Unless a community can address every page on the Internet individually, Smith may not be able to ascertain if he is violating the law by visiting certain pages.

This exposes the basic problem of obscenity. What is obscene to Smith may not be obscene to Smith's neighbor. This problem may possibly be eliminated if Smith just errs on the safe side to avoid prosecution. Thus, Smith could simply avoid all nudity and sites with any sexual content. However, this would greatly limit the usefulness of the Internet and Smith's confusion would continue. Smith may wish to learn about breast cancer by visiting a site that contains pictures of women before and after undergoing mastectomies. Clearly this site contains nudity. To err on the safe side would destroy access to this site and others containing useful material. In other words, this approach would have a dreadful silencing effect. Also, Smith may encounter a page which he believes does not contain anything that could be considered purely sexual in nature; however, his neighbor could come away from the page with an entirely different impression. Therefore, not only would such a conservative approach silence much Internet content, it would also still be too subjective to be reasonably employed.

Of course, community regulation of this sort would be mostly unnecessary. Unless, a viewer of Internet obscenity wishes to project an image onto a billboard, looking at Internet obscenity is, basically, a private activity. Any public display of such images could, reasonably, be dealt with by existing regulations on public advertising or other, similar ordinances. Therefore, it is not unreasonable that a community can insist that a person not view Internet obscenity using a large monitor in public parks or in government buildings. This is because in these cases, a person can err on the safe side without chilling speech by simply viewing Internet content in a more private location. However, the question arises once again if a community can regulate the private viewing of such materials. I believe the answer is clearly no.

While it is true that there exists legislation that is paternalistic and/or moralistic[89] in character, much of this legislation is slowly fading away. In the case of obscenity viewing, enacting such legislation would be unreasonable for many reasons previously discussed. Perhaps the most dramatic reason involves the silencing effect that such legislation would have due to the subjectivity involved in defining obscenity. In addition, passing such legislation in a country such as the United States would fly in the face of prior standards set for obscenity. While legal precedents do, sometimes, need to be amended and it would be a mistake to use the descriptive fact that they exist to make a normative claim, I believe that they have, for the most part, been enacted based on sound justifications. The basic justification is the liberty of persons to engage in activities of their choosing as long as such activities do not harm others.

In this chapter I have exposed many failings of the current obscenity standard in the United States as applied to Internet materials. Clearly, applying such legislation to Internet materials is hopelessly subjective and unworkable. Moreover, enforcement of such regulation, given its community-based standard, would be ad hoc and unjust. This is, I believe, a case where it is impossible to fit current technological methods of communication into already existent molds. Internet obscenity forces us to abandon these molds and either (a) make new ones or (b) abandon using molds altogether.

3

Why Free Speech Alone Should Not Protect Internet Obscenity and Pornography

Introduction

The freedom to say what one wishes is a negative liberty which many writers claim should be afforded special governmental protections. In fact, many commentators on this subject claim that there is, or should be, a right to free speech. Arguments advocating such protection are often made in the United States where there exists constitutional protection for freedom of speech. The First Amendment of the United States Constitution reads, "[C]ongress shall make no law respecting an establishment of religion, or prohibiting the free exercise thereof; or abridging the freedom of speech, or of the press; or the right of the people peaceably to assemble, and to petition the government for a redress of grievances."[1] Most arguments against Internet regulation of obscenity and pornography focus on the common justifications given for this First Amendment protection. In fact, many advocates of freedom of speech simply cite the United States Constitution.[2] However, merely appealing to the Constitution is an appeal to authority. While this is not inappropriate in legal matters within the United States, it fails to answer the question of why freedom of speech *should* be protected.

In this chapter I will present common arguments as to why Internet obscenity and pornography, and speech in general, should be protected. These arguments will be drawn primarily from philosophical ethics and social and political philosophy. Most of the arguments can be traced back to John Stuart Mill but have been developed by many authors. In this chapter I will suggest that these arguments are simply not enough to justify refraining from abridgment of cyber-speech.[3] Specifically, I will argue that the common justifications given for protecting speech are (a) flawed and (b) not applicable to most sexually explicit Internet materials. I am offering this double argument to avoid isolated examples that support a common argument or provide an example of sexually explicit material that may be covered by one of the common arguments.

The Appeal to Authority and Definition of Speech

Opponents of Internet regulation sometimes appeal to what those who framed the First Amendment had in mind when constructing it. This appeal centers on the question, "what would our founding fathers have thought?" This question is commonly addressed in current political speeches and debates. Even the diaries of Thomas Jefferson[4] and the autobiography of Benjamin Franklin[5] have been analyzed in attempts to gain a better understanding of their intentions. However, as Alexander Meiklejohn writes, the "Constitution derives whatever validity, whatever meaning it has not from its acceptance by our forefathers ... but from its acceptance by us now."[6] Some authors, such as Meiklejohn, have claimed that the First Amendment is an absolute imperative and that it "forbids Congress from making any law which shall abridge the freedom of speech."[7] Meiklejohn writes, "it is unqualified ... it admits of no exceptions."[8] Most other writers admit to exceptions to the First Amendment. Some of the most famous exceptions have long histories. In 1919, mainly due to the arguments made by Justice Oliver Wendell Holmes, the Supreme Court ruled that speech that would likely cause "clear and present danger" should not be constitutionally protected.[9] Today many regulations on speech are considered justified by the Court in the United States. For example, there are many instances where the United States court system has ruled that a right to free speech does not include speech acts such as perjury, extortion, libel, false advertising, or threatening bodily violence.[10] Also, as was previously discussed, obscenity is not legally considered a protected form of speech. Thus, the absolutist language of the Constitution is, in practice, severely weakened in the United States.

Following the Court's example, few proponents of freedom of speech believe that *all* speech should be free. Most writers on the subject acknowledge the necessity of suppressing speech in matters of national security. Also, few supporters of free speech would extend coverage to allow cigarette manufactures to print on a carton of regular unfiltered cigarettes, "this product does not contain tar or nicotine" or the owner of a trained attack dog to yell, "Kill!" at any time. In fact, most supporters of free speech agree that there should be some regulation. While there is debate about what should and should not be allowed, there is little argument that everything should be allowed.

Before embarking on arguments given for freedom of speech, it is important to specify what counts as speech. Proponents and opponents of a free speech principle typically try to define what they believe speech should include; however, this is not a light task. Speech, in writings on the subject, has been taken to have many diverse meanings. It has been characterized as self-expression, linguistic expression and communication. Self-expression is an external manifestation of inner feelings. Self-expression can be done in a painting, poem or even a scream. In fact, people can express themselves through almost any form of voluntary conduct. Given the diversity of self-expression, defining speech as such provides a definition that is simply too broad to be useful. This is because all action is self-expression to some extent. On the other hand, defining speech as linguistic expression does not capture many things that should reasonably be considered speech. Examples include the symbols used to express words, like Morse code and Braille. Of course, the definition could be modified to include those symbols that have a direct linguistic equivalent and thus would include the aforementioned examples. However, even with this modification, symbols such as a peace sign, which clearly has communicative content, would be excluded. Also, there are forms of expression that may not be candidates for speech. Such examples are screams or a shrill utterance of a single word executed solely in order to prevent someone else from being heard.

The most commonly used definition of speech is as communication and, given its commonality and the aforementioned problems with alternative definitions, it is the definition I will employ.[11] Communication involves conveying or attempting to convey a message from one person to another (or many others).[12] This is a joint enterprise. Without communicative intent, a communicated message and a recipient of the message, a communicative act is not complete. However, even with this definition, there are difficulties involved in determining what is speech. One problem is that speech is never pure. That is, any speech is accompanied by some action. This action may be subject to regulation even if the speech in question is not. For example, talking may cause noise, distribution of pamphlets may cause litter and a public demonstration may block traffic. However, even with these difficulties, the definition still remains useful as there are many cases that are clearly communicative or not, and it is, generally, clear. Now that a definition is in place, I will examine the common arguments for granting speech a special protected status.

Speech and Truth

Perhaps the most predominant and historically significant argument for affording speech a special protected status is that speech leads to the discovery of truth. In other words, a free and open discussion is the best way to arrive at truth. This argument appears in Milton's *Areopagitica* and is elaborated on by John Stuart Mill in *On Liberty*. Forms of the argument have also been used by United States Supreme Court justices such as Oliver Wendell Holmes who claimed that the best test of truth is the power of the thought to get itself accepted in the competition of the market.[13] In all of its forms this argument treats freedom of speech not as an end in itself, but only as a means of identifying and accepting truth. Thus, truth is a desired goal that is, in and of itself, valuable. The argument is intuitively appealing and most everyone can agree that truth is desirable. While I will not argue that truth is not a desired end, the argument is not without objections and does not apply to most obscenity and pornography on the Internet.

The argument from truth assumes that a marketplace of ideas is more likely to lead to truth than nonsense or widespread belief in falsehoods. However, most proponents of this argument do not offer a causal link between the marketplace and an abundance of truth. Of course, the method of establishing this connection will depend largely on how "truth" is defined. If the possibility of obtaining objective knowledge is rejected and truth is defined by a subjective standard, the causal link is easy to establish. If truth becomes nothing more than what survives in a marketplace of ideas or what works the best, it is, of course, necessary to provide such a marketplace for truth to emerge. However, if this conception of truth is utilized, the argument is plainly flawed. The most obvious flaw using this definition of truth is that the argument is circular. This is because the conclusion is assumed in the premises. Also, if truth is defined by what survives best as a process, why is free speech preferable to any other process? Without independent criteria for truth, there is no reason to prefer one process (such as authoritarian fiat) to another for establishing "truth." There is no rationale as to why we should prefer a marketplace of ideas to any other accepted situation. Thus, for this argument to be plausible, it must take a different epistemic stance. John Stuart Mill gives an example of such a stance. Mill believes that there is a real Truth to be found and advanced.

In *On Liberty* Mill attempts to establish a causal link between the free market of ideas and epistemic advance. Mill claims that the link is a product of our own fallibility. Only if we have the complete liberty to contradict a position are we justified in accepting its truth. If we were to hold that any of our beliefs were absolutely true, we would be assuming infallibility. Clearly no human is infallible. Given this fallibility, there is a possibility that, if any belief is suppressed, it may be true.[14] Because any belief may be false, suppressing any opposing belief entails suppressing a possibly true belief or suppressing a belief that is partially true.[15] Only by allowing an open discussion, Mill claims, do we allow for the possibility that these true beliefs will be expressed. Thus, Mill argues that a policy of suppressing beliefs will, in fact, suppress some true ones and thus impede the search for truth. This argument is clearly strong when the speech being suppressed is assumed to be false. However, there are times when the possibility of a belief being true has little to do with the reasons for suppressing it. In fact, there may be cases where beliefs are suppressed *because* they are thought to be *true*.

Consider, the studies detailed in the book by Richard Herrnstein and Charles Murray, *The Bell Curve: Intelligence and Class Structure in American Life*.[16] These studies claim that African Americans are less intelligent than Caucasian Americans. If the studies are reliable, there may be good reasons to suppress them *because* they may offer true information.[17] The possibility that truth is not being advanced by suppressing this evidence is relevant but may not be a priority. If such speech, if true, were not suppressed, discrimination could occur that would hinder a liberal interest in equality. Thus, the interest in suppressing the effects that such speech may cause may be greater than the interest in truth. In fact, if the discovery of truth is enough to justify free speech in all cases, truth must be more valuable than all other interests given in support of regulating speech.

This is relevant when we consider that expressions of belief often produce negative consequences. One risk of such expression is that the public will accept a false belief, as was the case in Nazi Germany. By the charismatic nature of Hitler's speeches and governmental control of media, many Germans were convinced that Jewish persons deserved a lesser status than others. Once accepted, there is also a risk that persons will act upon those beliefs, as was also the case in Nazi Germany. Even if not accepted by the general public, expression of belief can have unpleasant consequences. People may be offended, violence may be provoked and harm may arise from expressed belief. In these cases, it is important to consider if the possible increase in truth is worth the consequences produced. Given Mill's utilitarianism, the consequence of great disutility being produced would be unacceptable. Unless truth is a value above all,[18] the answer is certainly not clear. In many cases, the risk of harm involved may be quite significant. In these situations the question may be: is it worth taking a large risk that harm will occur due to the slight possibility that truth will be advanced? To give a positive answer assumes truth's lexical priority.

Another question which is relevant is, does truth really prevail in an arena of many beliefs? In other words, is an arena of free speech the best environment for truth to emerge? Most academic disciplines, in principle, presuppose a type of view similar to what Mill and proponents of the argument for truth envision.[19] By free discussion and exposure to many views, the disciplines assume that truth has a better chance of prevailing than in environments with limited exposure and discussion. Thus, in academia, the argument from truth seems to gain strength. However, even if truth is likely to prevail among academics, who are trained to reason rationally and chosen through selective processes for their ability to think in such a fashion, this does not necessitate that the same process will be effective in society at large. The argument from truth has the optimism of the Enlightenment. In the 18th and 19th centuries, there was a widespread belief that man was a rational creature and that if his mind was trained and liberated from superstition by education, he would always distinguish truth from falsehood and good from evil. We cannot share this faith today. History and modern psychology provide many examples where falsities have triumphed over truth, even in an arena of free speech. In fact, additional information can certainly retard epistemic advance. In a haystack of false statements, the needle of truth may be hard to find. Also, the power of deception can be very strong. Since Plato inveighed against the Sophists, the idea that deception can lead one to believe almost anything has been recognized. Thus, the advancement of truth may depend more on the rhetorical power of its advocate than a marketplace of ideas.

Even if the argument from truth were sound, for many materials on the Internet, truth is not a primary concern. For example, while there may be reasons for allowing someone in Hyde Park to yell that the moon is made of cream cheese, truth can hardly be one. Another example is Oliver Wendell Holmes' famous case of a man yelling "fire" in a crowded theater.[20] In this case, it would be foolish to argue that he should be permitted to express himself because some truth could be gained from his utterance. The same is true for most pornography and obscenity on the Internet. For such materials I believe the question of truth is simply not relevant as a reason for protection.[21] What, it may be asked, is the truth that is to be gained from a picture depicting bestiality? The truth argument has a limited scope and simply should not cover most Internet obscenity and pornography.[22] The recognition of this limited scope can be seen in current regulations against defamation and misrepresentation. If I advertised for sale an ancient Egyptian Shabti from the Late Kingdom but, in fact, was selling a reproduction made a little over a month ago, protecting my speech based on the argument from truth would be dubious indeed. Also, if I spread falsehoods against a local doctor in writing over the Internet, he could rightfully claim that his character was defamed and order their removal. Given this limitation and the previously mentioned problems with the argument from truth, I believe it is clear that if sexually explicit Internet materials should be protected, the justification for such protection will have to be found elsewhere. In the next section I will examine two further common arguments that claim to provide such a justification.

The Arguments from Autonomy and Dignity

The arguments from autonomy and dignity share similar structures. The argument from autonomy claims that autonomy is good and that freedom of speech is a necessary condition for autonomy to emerge. Therefore, it is claimed that freedom of speech is good because of its relationship to autonomy.[23] The argument from dignity centers on the fact that autonomous individuals should be afforded dignity and space to exercise their autonomy. Because humans should have dignity and be afforded respect (which includes the ability to exercise their autonomy in speech), this argument claims that restricting freedom of speech is simply not a role that a democratic government should have over free and autonomous citizens.

Human dignity has been much discussed in recent ethical and political theory, most notably by John Rawls.[24] Implicit in Rawls' contractarian justification for freedom of speech is the idea that persons possess dignity and should be free and equal.[25] The best way for such equality to be expressed, according to Rawls, is if persons try to place themselves in an "original position." This position is a hypothetical situation in which people of roughly equal ability agree on principles of social cooperation without knowing how anybody is placed in society. In order for this position to be achieved, individuals must put themselves behind a "veil of ignorance," to ensure that they do not know where they will be placed in the resulting society. Behind the veil people will not know their class, race, or sex and will act impartially (or as close to it as possible). Rawls argues that all parties behind such a veil would insist on a strong priority for basic liberties, including freedom of speech.[26] This is because they would not want to risk something so important on the luck of where they might be placed in society. Thus, starting from the foundations of dignity and fairness, a justification is given for freedom of speech and other basic liberties.[27] However, this argument is not sufficient to justify a principle of free speech. One flaw is that restricting many actions can be as much of a hindrance to individual liberties as restricting speech. Both restrictions can be seen as affronts to human dignity. Thus, proponents of this argument must hold that restricting speech assaults human dignity more than restricting actions. One way to support this claim is to argue that speech is personal and more of a representation of a person than actions. After all, speech is the most direct way of communicating to others who we are.

While this is reasonable, it is also true that many types of actions are also deeply integral to who we are. In fact, some actions such as those associated with sexual intimacy, religious rituals, and many others may also constitute who we are (perhaps more than speech). Restrictions on these intimate actions will assault dignity as much, if not more, than regulations on speech. Therefore, this argument fails to carve out the special status for speech apart from actions that proponents of a free speech principle desire.[28]

Another formulation on the dignity argument appeals to the autonomy of the hearer and not of the speaker. Thomas Scanlon outlined this argument in several of his writings.[29] In short, the argument claims that because we are beings with dignity (for Scanlon, a free individual), there are certain things that we should not be protected from. One of these things is speech and the possibility of hearing falsehoods. As Scanlon writes, "The harm of coming to have false beliefs is not one that an autonomous man could allow the state to protect him against."[30]

This appeal to the dignity and autonomy of the hearer resonates well with the idea of what it means to be an individual living in a society that values freedom and autonomy. However, this formulation suffers much the same fate as the argument from dignity that focuses on the speaker. In short, it does not justify a special status for speech. Also, Scanlon himself has realized that the argument is overdrawn.[31] There are certainly some false beliefs (triggered by speech) that it is reasonable to be protected against. A possible example is the false belief that smoking cigarettes does not cause cancer. Other possibilities abound in cases of false advertising where an average citizen may not have the tools to verify such claims at their ready disposal. For example, suppose citizen Smith wants to visit a dentist to have a root canal performed. Citizen Smith sees an advertisement in his local newspaper for Dentist Quack that states that the dentist is board certified and has received a dental degree. However, if it turns out to be the case that Dentist Quack has never received dental training and is not board certified the autonomy of citizen Smith is certainly not a sufficient reason for allowing the false speech contained in the advertisement. These examples need not be limited to commercial advertisements. For example, if scientist Jones discovered that an asteroid was likely to destroy the Earth in a matter of days and nothing could be done to stop the asteroid or protect the Earth's inhabitants, there might be good reasons to protect persons from this knowledge. Such protection could make the final days of the Earth's population more pleasurable without the knowledge of their impending deaths. In this case it is quite possible that the autonomy of a potential listener could be outweighed by the disutility produced by the assertion of such knowledge.

Autonomy[32] has emerged in many modern ethical theories as a good.[33] In fact, in some modern ethical theories, autonomy has emerged as *the* most important good. The argument from autonomy claims that only by affording people the opportunity to explore opinions through freedom of discussion will they truly develop independent judgments and make autonomous decisions. Only in this way will we come to know who we truly are, proponents of this argument claim. Thus, freedom of speech is good because it allows for the development of autonomous individuals. While it is clear that a person need not hear all speech to be autonomous, the claim is merely that freedom of speech provides the raw materials to allow autonomy to flourish. While he never uses the word *autonomy*, this is similar to an argument offered by Mill.

While Mill's *On Liberty* relies heavily on the argument from truth, more than truth is involved in his justification for freedom of speech. Mill claims that if people fail to engage in thought and discussion or understand why their beliefs are justified they will merely be dogmatic. Thus, there is more than truth discovery at work here. Freedom of speech is a necessary condition for person building at the level of beliefs. Engaging in discussion allows individuals to be exposed to a variety of views and decide what they believe, not just what they have been told to believe. This is the foundation for making autonomous decisions. Therefore, according to Mill, for a person to build character and to become an autonomous agent, he or she must have access to free speech. While this belief building is not identical with furthering autonomy in individuals, the claim being made is that it is useful and helps individuals become more autonomous. Thus, free expression is a type of mental gymnastics with which to build autonomous citizens.[34]

As previously mentioned, Mill is certainly not alone is making assertions linking speech and autonomy. Thomas Scanlon writes, an "autonomous person cannot accept without independent consideration the judgment of others as to what he should believe or what he should do."[35] Before Scanlon and Mill, Spinoza drew a connection between mental autonomy and freedom of speech in *Tractatus Theologico-Politicus*.[36] This is also the common model of a liberal education. For example, in a course on ethics, most professors expose their students to many conflicting views. This is because the purpose of such a class is not to replace a set of beliefs with another but to present a broad spectrum to allow for autonomous decisions to be made.

Although the argument from autonomy gains support by educational models and intuitive appeal, I believe it is insufficient to justify a special status for speech. While freedom of speech may allow for mental gymnastics, it is not effectual if the general population is unable or unwilling to exercise in such a fashion. Gymnastics on a balance beam may be wonderful exercise for those who can do it, but not for those who fall off and injure themselves. The argument from autonomy suffers one of the same flaws as the argument from truth and simply may not be effective for the general populace.[37] While it may be possible that exposure to speech can build autonomy, it is also possible that such exposure will cause persons to close themselves off and become narrowly focused. Also, this argument from autonomy can be objected to on the grounds that restrictions on actions also affect individual autonomy and decision making. One may need to experience certain actions in order to make informed choices. This is especially true in cases involving likes and dislikes. In order to know if I like X, I often need to experience X. Further, my knowledge of my like or dislike of X may influence my other decisions. Thus, if I am never able to experience X, my decisions, which could be influenced by this knowledge, are also impaired. Of course this need not be the case for all actions. For example, I probably would not jump off a cliff to test if I like it. This would be due to past experiences with pain and being hurt. Knowing that being hurt is a probable outcome of falling from a cliff, I would be able to conclude, without actually experiencing it, that I do not want to fall. However, this would not tell me if I liked the sensation of falling. I could, however, jump off the same cliff with a cord attached to my leg to find out if I liked the sensation provided by jumping off cliffs. Also, there are clear cases where one has to experience something to know if one likes it. Jones will never know if he likes the Indian dish baingan bharta unless he samples the dish. In fact, it could be the case that baingan bharta would be Jones' favorite dish if he sampled it. However, unless he eats the dish, he will never know the gustatory joy. Therefore, the argument from autonomy is not satisfactory in providing a justification as to why speech should be given a special status that actions do not merit.[38]

Speech and Democracy

Another possible justification for freedom of speech in a country such as the United States revolves around the idea that such a freedom is beneficial and, perhaps, even necessary for democracy to properly function. Although many separate arguments have been offered supporting this theme,[39] I will merge them due to their common overarching claim that freedom of speech is necessary for a democracy to function (at least function well). It is worth mention that most formulations of the argument from democracy are somewhat similar to the argument from autonomy and assume that freedom of speech is autonomy-enhancing.

Democracy, in its ideal form, assumes that it is the citizens who are sovereign. In order to be sovereign and for democracy to function, the individuals in a democracy must be informed and autonomously make decisions. Even if the members of a democracy ultimately decide that they are happy electing representatives to make decisions, this is still a decision that, ideally, is made autonomously. It has been argued that for individuals to be their own lawmakers they have to know what they believe and have access to relevant information. This is the argument given by Meiklejohn: in order to rule oneself, one must know oneself. Meiklejohn writes:

> We [United States citizens] listen, not because of the desire to speak, but because we need to hear. If there are arguments against our theory of government, our policies in war or in peace, we the citizens, the rulers, must hear and consider them for ourselves. That is the way of public safety, it is the program of self-government.[40]

Meiklejohn claims that persons in a democracy ideally need the First Amendment to protect their right to hear what is said and to allow for true self-government. Meiklejohn believes that only by such protection can we guarantee that every voting citizen can hear all sides and make autonomous decisions. He writes, "[W]hen a free man is voting, it is not enough that the truth is known by some legislator. The voters must have it, all of them."[41] Therefore, free speech becomes a foundational rock on which democracy stands.

This argument is entirely reasonable and, in an ideal democracy, there should be freedom of political speech. Of course, the arguments for freedom of speech based on democracy require the prior acceptance of democratic ideals. Thus, the extent to which this argument can be accepted is limited. However, in the United States, it is reasonable to assume that most citizens do uphold such principles. Given this, the argument seems to be thoroughly applicable and a sensible justification for upholding a special status for speech in the United States.

However, on further inspection, it becomes clear that this argument only protects a certain kind of speech: political speech. Using Meikle-john's definition, political (or public) speech is speech that discusses the public interest.[42] Meiklejohn embraces this distinction, and he dis-tinguishes between speech that should be protected (absolutely) and speech that should not. He claims that there are two "radically different kinds of utterances."[43] Given this, he acknowledges the fact that only public speech can be protected under his argument. Clearly some forms of expression are not political. Indeed, it would be dubious to attempt to defend access to hard core pornography based on the fact that voters may not be able to make autonomous political decisions without access. Also, a page on latex fetishes can hardly be considered political speech. Given this non-political speech, the argument from democracy does not provide the depth of coverage needed to afford special status to much speech. For example: although some pictures do have political content, such as Picasso's *Guernica*, many do not and would not be covered by any argument that appeals to democracy.

In fact, it can be questioned if some material often labeled as pro-tected by free speech enthusiasts on First Amendment grounds is cov-ered by any justification for free speech. For example, assuredly the existence of hard core pornography is not covered by any arguments previously discussed. Hard core pornography is closer to a sexual aid than speech.[44] The vendor of such materials is selling a product for the specific purpose of inducing sexual stimulation without communica-tive intent. This is clearly not communication that is protected by any arguments commonly given to justify a free speech principle. Thus, rely-ing only on the First Amendment or a principle of free speech for pro-tection of such material is simply unconvincing.

The Negative Argument: A Slippery Slope

The arguments covered thus far have given positive justifications for freedom of speech; however, negative justifications have also been made in the literature. In other words, many authors have pointed out not that freedom of speech has a special value, but that regulating speech leads to undesirable consequences. Throughout history there have been many acts of regulation that, looking back, are clearly abhorrent.[45] Given this history, the negative argument for freedom of speech claims that experience illustrates that governments are not particularly worthy censors. Thus, it is claimed that governments should not censor for fear of repeating past mistakes. Phil Cox writes of granting the state regulatory power: "censorship is a double futility. It cannot prevent any single intended criticism; and is bound to suspect a theoretically infinite number of unintended ones." Cox continues, "Pre-cyber history certainly abounds with such examples of abuse; one only need take a cursory look at recent initiatives to control cyber speech to witness the same danger, when the genie is let out."[46]

This argument continues on to a slippery slope and claims that if some things are censored, it will open the way for many other materials to fall prey to censorship. Proponents imagine society sliding down the slope until the government censors speech that clearly should be unregulated. This argument is quite old and can be seen throughout history. For example, Lord Chesterfield, stating his opinion on the Theatres Act of 1737, claimed:

> There is such a connection between licentiousness and liberty, that it is not easy to correct the one, without dangerously wounding the other. It is extremely hard to distinguish the true limit between them; like a changeable silk, we can easily see there are two different colors, but we cannot easily discover where the one ends, or where the other begins.[47]

More recently Joel Feinberg has expressed this position. Of this, Feinberg writes, "surely if there is one thing that is not infallibly known, it is how to draw the line" between what is acceptable and what is not.[48] However, arguments of this type are notoriously defective (although there are some quite effective ones) as they can be used to justify slipping down the slope in either direction. Using the same historical background, it is sometimes possible to argue both A and ~A using a slippery slope argument. For example, a similar argument has been made which leads to a conclusion that is the opposite of the previous argument. Robert Bork makes such an argument when he claims that if we start tolerating some speech we will soon tolerate harmful speech until we are "slouching towards Gomorrah."[49] In other words, by drawing on the same historical evidence, Bork claims that speech regulations will become too permissive (or nonexistent), not too restrictive. In fact, supporters of this position could point towards the toleration of Internet "filth" as a gigantic leap down the slippery slope. Thus, it is possible that a slippery slope argument as, or even more, convincing can be made in the other direction.

For a slippery slope to be effective there must be some reason provided as to why it is inevitable or likely that the slippage will occur past a certain point. Also, it is necessary to illustrate why it will not slide the other way. Proponents of the negative argument have, I believe, failed to satisfy both of these conditions. Therefore, this argument suffers from the weakness of many slippery slopes and is ineffective at justifying a special protected status for speech.

Speech and Action?

Even if the arguments for freedom of speech were valid and not limited in scope, it is difficult to distinguish much speech from action. People can communicate in various ways. Wearing a shirt with a peace sign may be a form of communication[50] as well as an action. In fact, endeavoring to distinguish speech from action is assuredly difficult. One's actions, tattoos, dress and even hair length certainly communicate something about the person having or wearing these items. In many cases, people communicate through picketing, demonstrating and other expressive acts. Speech is itself composed of actions, and most speech is intended to produce some response in the form of an action or other speech. Given these ambiguities, it would be elegantly simple to hold all speech protected regardless of the content. This position would mesh nicely with a general distrust of the government to censor speech. However, this is not a plausible position. There is communication that has nothing to do with the justifications provided for free speech. Also, to protect some of this communication may cause great harm.

Even staunch proponents of a principle of free speech treat some forms of speech outside the coverage of the principle. An example is Meiklejohn's exclusion of private speech. Such cases of exclusion are often referred to as "speech plus."[51] If examined, these distinctions are often unclear; however, they do point to a general pattern. The pattern is that if enough harm is produced by speech, it should be regulated. Famous examples such as shouting "fire" in a crowded theater given by Holmes and Mill's corn-dealer example[52] are often thought to fit this pattern. Given this, some authors have stated a free speech principle as "restrictions on speech should be permitted only when the restrictions cannot be avoided."[53] However, this sounds remarkably like a principle that should, in a liberal society, apply to both actions and speech.

The Political Alternative and Objections

Given the failure of the aforementioned arguments we are left with only political speech as possibly meriting a special status outside the ordinary operation of the harm principle. However, some authors have mounted objections to this conclusion. In *Free Speech in an Open Society* Rodney Smolla argues that the belief that only political speech merits heightened protection is "illogical and unconvincing."[54] He writes, "[T]here are at least four sound reasons to treat self-governance as *a* rationale for specially protected speech, but not as *the* exclusive rationale."[55] Smolla's four reasons are as follows:

1. Nonpolitical speech is not intrinsically less valuable than political speech
2. Self-governance theory[56] does not demand exclusivity
3. Any topic in modern life may bear some relation to self-governance
4. The claim that only speech useful to the government should be protected is elitist[57]

While the first claim is true, it has nothing to do with granting a right to free speech. There are many things in life that may be valuable, but that does not lead to the conclusion that there should be a special right to them. The second claim is also true. However, again, it implies nothing. Just as there is nothing in a self-governance argument that demands exclusivity, there is nothing that prevents it. Claim four seems to be simply false (almost by definition). How could a principle of self-governance be elitist when it is all citizens who ideally govern? Further, this principle does not imply that people do not say things that are important and non-political.

Smolla's third point is his strongest. Certainly it is true that a citizen takes more than just strictly political speech into consideration when making decisions in regard to self-governance In fact, a citizen may draw strongly on past experiences with many forms of speech when making political decisions. As discussed previously, there are shades of gray in what counts as political speech. Also, people try to influence political processes and decisions in many ways. Some of these are subtle and may not be immediately recognizable as political speech. Given this ambiguity, Smolla could be correct in his criticism.

Although Smolla's third objection is more reasonable than those that proceed and follow, it is still seriously flawed. While it is true that a voter might take non-political speech into account when making a decision in regard to self-governance, this does not lead to the conclusion that it is wrong to only protect political speech or that all speech should be protected. A person may draw on a wide variety of speech as well as experiences when voting; however, it would be unwise to argue that all things that could influence a political decision should be outside the normal operations of the harm principle. In addition, while there are some shades of gray, there are also clear blacks and whites in regard to a definition of political speech. A centerfold in *Playboy* magazine is clearly not political speech, nor is a picture of a woman having sexual relations with a dog. On the other hand, a congressional report is clearly political in nature. Given that there are clear cases, the existence of hard cases does not make the definition useless.

In this chapter I have outlined common rationales given for a principle of free speech and have shown that they can not logically be used to protect sexually explicit Internet materials. Given the failure of the aforementioned arguments, I conclude that Internet obscenity and pornography should not be insulated from the considerations of competing interests. If the harm caused by regulating sexually explicit

Internet materials is less than the harm these materials produce, they should be regulated in the interests of utility. In the chapters that follow I will examine arguments to the effect that such materials are, indeed, harmful.

4

Harm to Children

Introduction

Perhaps the most common argument for regulating pornography and obscenity on the Internet is that such material can harm children. This concern was expressed in the Exon-Coats Communications Decency Act. As Senator Exon writes of the act: "it stands for the simple premise that it is wrong to provide pornography to children on computers just as it is wrong to do it on a street corner or anywhere else."[1] This argument is appealing because it is horrific to imagine innocent children being harmed.

The Supreme Court, in *Reno v. ACLU*, validated a governmental interest in "protecting children." Also, Congressional Representative Michael G. Oxley from Ohio claimed, in a hearing addressing legislative proposals to protect children from inappropriate materials on the Internet, that "protecting kids from the degrading content readily available on the internet is the most serious threat to morality that we face."[2] The commitment to the protection of children from sexually explicit materials was stated as a justification for the Child Online Protection Act (COPA) in the United States. COPA, which made the distribution on the Internet of any material that is harmful to minors illegal, was signed into law on October 21, 1998. Less than twenty-four hours later, COPA was challenged[3] and on February 1, 1999, a preliminary injunction blocking enforcement of the law was issued. The United States Supreme Court decided to uphold the injunction in the much-publicized case of *Ashcroft v. ACLU*, however, the case is set to be appealed again. Clearly there is a governmental and social interest in the protection of children and, if unregulated Internet obscenity and pornography unnecessarily harms them, this would be grounds to consider regulation.

History and the Current Standard

In a general form, the harm to children argument has a long history and has been used to justify the regulation of television and radio and the addition of warning labels on music recordings. Senator Joseph Lieberman, who lobbied for warning labels on music recordings and video games, said in a press conference, "[W]e are in fact treating media like tobacco and other products that pose a risk to our children."[4] The view, expressed by Lieberman, that sexual materials put children at risk is widespread in the United States. In 1996, the United States Congress appropriated $250 million for sexual education programs in the United States. However, in order to receive funding, programs were required to teach that until marriage only abstinence was permissible. Programs were also required to advocate the view that "sexual activity outside of the context of marriage is likely to have harmful psychological and physical effects."[5] Programs were also forbidden from discussing safer sex or contraception.

Currently, in the United States, the Federal Communications Commission (FCC) regulates public broadcasts and it is unlawful to sell pornography to minors. Also, the right to distribute to minors any "indecent" material is, legally, very limited. While non-obscene material is, technically, protected speech, it is not so if distributed to a minor. This is clear in *Ginsberg v. New York* where the United States Supreme Court affirmed the conviction of a defendant[6] who distributed material considered harmful to minors.[7] In this case, the Court found that there exists a compelling interest in protecting the welfare of children and that a state can bar the distribution of indecent material to children (even material which is not obscene to adults). The harm to children argument appeals to what most parents have an interest in: ensuring that their children remain unharmed. To help in this quest, the United

States legal system now uses a "harmful to minors" standard. The standard assumes that what is harmful[8] to minors is what is obscene to minors. Of course this is question begging because it merely assumes that obscenity is harmful but bases what is harmful on what is obscene. Thus we are left with a circular argument that what is obscene is that which is harmful and that which is harmful is what is obscene. Given that the "harmful to minors" standard is a subset of the current obscenity standards in the United States, the definition used to determine what is obscene or harmful is virtually identical to that set forth in *Miller v. California*.[9] The only difference is that children are now used as the reference point. Thus, the new three-prong test insists that for material to be harmful or obscene the following conditions must be true:

1. The material's content must appeal to the prurient[10] interests of children,
2. The material must be patently[11] offensive to children, and
3. The material must lack significant social, literary, scientific, or political value for children.

Even with this new standard and definition of what is obscene to children and, thus, harmful to minors, the argument based on harm to children still lacks a substantial foundation.

One of the reasons the harm to children standard fails to be adequate is that it is, as is the adult obscenity standard, community based. As was argued in Chapter Two, this can be quite a problem because communities, or even individuals, certainly do not agree on what is obscene. This community dependence has been the case historically and will probably continue to be the case. Verdi often wrote different librettos to fit different community standards because his operas were considered indecent in some communities and not others.[12] While Verdi's operas are no longer viewed as indecent or harmful, community standards are still variable and changing constantly. Just a few decades ago the song "Puff, the Magic Dragon" by Peter, Paul and Mary was seen as promoting drug use and considered harmful to minors. Also the song "Louie, Louie" by Richard Berry was investigated by the FCC under the accusation that when played at 78 rpm backwards it contained

71

a suggestive message that could be harmful to children.[13] Today, Australian censors ban naked breasts from display in magazines and billboards on the basis that it is harmful to children. However, in parts of Europe such nudity is considered neither harmful to children nor offensive to reasonable adults. What constitutes a minor is also context-sensitive. For example, in Australia, a minor is defined as someone under the age of fifteen; however, in the United States, many definitions of a minor include those under eighteen.[14] Given this dependence on community standards, the current "harmful to minors" standard, much like its adult counterpart, is subjective and, generally, unreasonable to use as a legal standard for Internet materials.

However, as with the adult obscenity standard, the fact that the current standard does not work does not indicate that no standard will. In what follows, I will explore the arguments to the effect that Internet pornography and obscenity should be regulated because they harm children. If harm is incurred, this will be reason to attempt to formulate a new standard. However, I will argue that the harm to children argument, in all its forms, fails to justify regulation of Internet pornography and obscenity. The reasons for this failure are numerous. Not only do proponents who claim harm occurs use a narrow definition of harm; they fail to show that any harm will occur.

The "Harm" in Harm to Children

Despite the notorious difficulties in determining what exactly constitutes harm, I will use Feinberg's definition of harm as a "wrongfully set-back interest."[15] In general, in order for an interest to be set back and harm to occur there must be evidence apart from the claim to harm that harm did, indeed, occur. This is the difference between harm and offense in broad terms. Even with this definition, it is often difficult to assess if an interest is impeded and to what extent an interest must be retarded (provided it is a "valid" interest) before regulation can occur. However, just because there are shades of gray in this definition, there are also clear blacks and whites and I believe that the definition remains useful. This is true of most descriptions. For example, the distinction between large, medium and small persons has shades of gray. Clearly if we encounter an individual who is almost seven feet tall and has clothes specially made to accommodate his enormous stature, he would be called large. There are also cases where it is not clear if a person is large or medium. However, these borderline cases do not make "large person" a useless description. I believe the same is true of harms. While there may be questionable cases, the term remains useful and, in a number of cases, it is clear whether harm does or does not occur.

Before I examine specific issues of concern for proponents of the harm to children argument, it is necessary to point out a basic flaw in most versions of the argument. Most proponents of the harm to children argument employ a definition of harm that is much too narrow for the situation. Simply, they assume that the transitory injury (if any occurs)[16] that may be caused by a child viewing sexually explicit Internet material is the level at which they should be evaluating harm. An example to clarify this situation involves two soldiers. Suppose there are two soldiers heading off into battle with the knowledge that their chances of survival are slim. Soldier A asks Soldier B to shoot her in the leg in order for her to be taken to the army infirmary and avoid the deadly battle. Clearly, if ever there were a clear case of a harm it would be in intentionally shooting someone; however, while it may be true that A did inflict an injury on B, if any injury is produced, it is outweighed by the benefits received. Therefore, no interest is wrongfully hindered and a net harm is not produced. Soldier A's interests are actually advanced rather than hindered. Similarly, while being exposed to certain materials *may* (or may not) cause a slight injury to children or adults, this may well be outweighed by the benefits incurred in having a global, uncensored communications medium. While the two situations mentioned may also be different for several reasons, the point remains that there are levels at which harm may be viewed. Moreover, as the example suggests, often that which produces a temporary injury does, ultimately, result in a net gain. Having an unregulated Internet might result in such a net benefit for society as a whole as well as any given individual (due to the benefit derived by living in such a society). In order to address this issue, proponents of the harm to children argument must make a convincing case that not only are children injured by a glance at pornography or obscenity but that, overall, their interests (both present and future interests being considered) are being wrongfully retarded. I will now examine the specific concerns of proponents of the harm to minors argument and demonstrate that they fail to prove that, overall, harm is caused In her best-selling book, *The Parent's Guide to Protecting Your Children in Cyberspace,* Parry Aftab outlines several risks to children (that is, risks to cause harm) on the Internet. Two of the main risks she considers deal specifically with obscenity and pornography. They are that children can access inappropriate information, and that children can be lured by cyber-predators who often engage in obscene chat or visit "adult" areas on the Internet. While she discusses these risks he fails to make an argument that they will, in fact, cause harm. This is probably not necessary as it seems intuitive that children *could* be harmed in these ways. However, riding a bike on a sidewalk or even walking down a street *could* also harm a child. The question that must be answered is if the harm that could be caused (if any harm is caused at all) is likely, substantial and not easily avoidable. I add easily avoidable because if it is easy to avoid a harm, given the disutility produced by regulation,[17] simply avoiding it will most likely lead to greater utility than regulation. Given this, I will consider if, indeed, any of Aftab's risks do cause likely, substantial and not easily avoidable harm.

Pedophiles and Perverts

Perhaps one of the most terrifying thoughts for parents is that there are perverts or pedophiles on the Internet waiting to lure children. Many proponents of the harm to children argument claim that children can, in fact, be lured by cyber-predators and that an unregulated Internet is an attractive area for such predators. As Stephen Wiley, the chief of the Violent Crimes and Major Offenders Section of the Federal Bureau of Investigation (FBI), states: "[T]his technology has allowed our nation's children to become vulnerable to exploitation and harm by pedophiles and other sexual predators."[18] This is a troubling thought, and proponents of censorship reinforce their arguments by citing cases where children have been lured or pedophiles have attempted to entice children by means of "obscene" chat. This is directly relevant to the regulation of Internet pornography because it is often claimed that it is on sites that feature sexually explicit chat and/or pictures that these predators make contact with their victims. Given these horrifying examples, proponents make it clear that regulation of such sites is desperately needed to prevent harm. One widely publicized cyber-predator case involved Patrick Green, a resident of the United Kingdom who was sentenced to five years in prison for having sex with a 13-year-old child he contacted over the Internet. Another often cited case is that involving Patrick Naughton, an Infoseek executive, who was arrested on a pier in Santa Monica, California, September 16, 1999, for soliciting sex with a minor. This "minor" was really a FBI agent posing as a 13-year-old girl named KrisLA. After chatting in the "Dad and Daughter Sex" chat room, Naughton agreed to meet KrisLA for a sexual encounter. Naughton was arrested where he had agreed to meet "the girl." This case is not unique, in fact, there have been many such documented cases where older men have tried to lure children into having sexual relations with them in chat rooms or by using other Internet resources.[19] If these Internet resources were regulated, proponents claim, such cases might not occur.

In fact, many have argued that the Internet is a breeding ground for perverts who use adult sites in search of potential victims and, because of this, sexually explicit Internet materials should, obviously, be regulated.[20] These cases, opponents argue, are plainly so heinous that anyone can ascertain that regulation is necessary.

I will not suggest that the aforementioned cases are moral; however, it is quite obvious that no child can be physically molested online. Children can only be physically molested offline; therefore, the Internet is only the communication method utilized. Propositioning a child is propositioning a child, on or off the Internet. To consistently argue for regulation of Internet pornography on the basis that it is an area attractive to child molesters and perverts would be to accept similar arguments for the closing of public swimming pools, malls, parks and other places child molesters may seek to entice their victims. As is the case in any public space, there will be persons of questionable character on the Internet; however, this does not lead to the conclusion that regulation is justified. While there exists a small percentage of criminals on the Internet, there is also a small percentage of criminals in most towns; however, this does not prevent us from letting children play in parks or go to shopping malls. This is true even when we know that most sexual abuse cases are not Internet related.

At this point, proponents of the harm to children argument may claim that the harm done to children by sexual predators on the Internet need not be physical. It may be possible that encounters with sexual predators which involve "nasty" talk may confuse and/or harm children psychologically. Given the ease of such encounters over the Internet, an argument could be constructed that regulation of the Internet is appropriate on these grounds. However, statistically, according to a leading children's rights campaigner and journalist, Larry Magid, when encountering others on the Internet, the greatest risk is that a child will encounter people in chat areas and news groups who are mean or obnoxious.[21] While it may be appropriate to police some of these spaces to prevent illegal actions from occurring, denying access to them is clearly not the answer. The possible harm involved here is the same as (or less than) in other public spaces. As is true in most public spaces, using parental supervision, and policing methods is likely to produce far less disutility than denying access to such areas.[22] Also, as I will argue later in this chapter, the claim that pornographic material psychologically harms children is unsupported.

Material Inappropriate for Children

The potential harm to children most often cited is that children can access inappropriate material. Concern about this access often arises because of the concern that sexually explicit materials can rob children of innocence. Under this view, children are innocent creatures; however, after a quick look at history and childhood psychosocial development, it is clear that this view is misguided.

The construction of the image of childhood innocence is a fairly recent and very Christian development. Boys in ancient Greece and Rome were often sexual partners for older mentors.[23] Children in these ancient societies were not considered innocent and little effort was made to keep sexually explicit materials from them. Christianity radically changed Western views and attitudes about sexual knowledge. With the Christian notion that sexual desire is often sinful, childhood protection from sexual materials assumed a spiritual value.[24] Virginity in girls was also often historically protected; however, this was due more to the female status as property than an assumed innocence.[25] However, the main construction of the concept of childhood innocence was an invention of the 17th century. Philippe Aries argues in his book, *Centuries of Childhood*, that until the 17th century "nobody thought that this innocence existed."[26] Aries concludes in his work that the creation of this unique idea of childhood innocence has taught children to conceal their bodies and produced anxieties that are with us today.

One of the consequences of the construction of childhood innocence is the view that masturbation is shameful. Shame and guilt are often foisted on youngsters who engage in this natural and common practice. In fact, during the 18th century, masturbation was claimed to cause a variety of ailments. These included jaundice, loose teeth, consumption, hysteria, impotence, tumors and insanity.[27] To prevent children from engaging in this "self-abuse," sexually explicit materials were kept from them and often other preventive measures were employed. Peter Gay writes of some of these preventive measures. Some measures were fairly mild, however, practices like cauterization of the sexual organs, infibulation, and even castration were used in persistent cases. Gay writes of some common methods, including "modern chastity belts for girls and ingenious penile rings for boys or straitjackets for both, all designed to keep growing or adolescent sinners from getting at themselves."[28] Even today masturbation is associated with shame and the myth of childhood innocence continues. In fact, the efforts to keep this sexual subject away from children even caused the former surgeon general, Joycelyn Elders, to be dismissed from office following her suggestion that sexual education should address masturbation.

Despite all this concern about lost innocence it may be, as the much-censored author Judy Blume writes, "children are inexperienced but, they are not innocent." Blume also makes a reasonable suggestion and claims, "[W]e cannot restore a 'lost innocence' that may have never existed at all, but we can offer perspectives from our experience and help interpreting the world, flaws and all."[29]

Harm and Exposure

The fear that childhood innocence will be lost by exposure to pornography is widespread and, as Howard Poole writes, "there seems to be substantial agreement on the need to protect children from obscene pornography."[30] Pornography[31] and obscenity are often conflated by the layperson; however, they are not the same. Nevertheless, some proponents of the harm to children argument claim that pornography is obscene for children. Thus, given that they believe exposure to obscenity is harmful to minors, pornography is harmful to minors. While this of course begs the question, it remains to be argued if, indeed, exposure to pornography on the Internet is harmful to children.

In support of the assertion that pornography is harmful to children, proponents often cite individual cases where they claim children have done horrible things after viewing pornography. Such claims are evident in the statement by Mary Anne Layden of the Center for Cognitive Therapy at the University of Pennsylvania. Layden recited to the House of Representatives, during a hearing on controlling inappropriate materials on the Internet, a case involving a boy who forced his sister to have sex with him after being exposed to pornography.[32] The boy, Frankie, was twelve and his sister, Cathy, was eight when they discovered their father's collection of pornography. Soon after, according to Layden, Frankie began to insist that his sister have sex with him. This behavior continued every night for 10 years. After this traumatic experience, Cathy became a nun and Frankie became a sex addict. According to Layden, this sex addiction caused, later in life, Frankie's marriage to dissolve and his children to disassociate from him.[33] In this same statement, Layden also stressed the seriousness of pornography and linked it to the nation's cocaine problem.[34] Layden says, "[T]hose of us who are treating the cross-addicted individual are finding that relapse into cocaine is happening through sex addiction." She continues, "[W]e will not get the cocaine problem in the country under control until we control sex addiction."[35] Given the lack of any supportive evidence linking sexual urges with cocaine addiction, this assertion is clearly dubious.

Many other proponents of this argument have also been very vocal. For example, due to the availability of pornography on the Internet, Republican senator Daniel Coats of Indiana claimed that the "Internet destroys innocence."[36] Also, many parents are simply uncomfortable with the possibility that their children could be exposed to pornography. Fears of anti-social behavior, sex addiction and loss of innocence are just a few reasons parents may wish to protect their children from pornography. Due to the ease of use and abundance of material on the Internet, these parental fears are magnified.

Children are renowned for their curiosity, and when their bodies start to change they want to know what is going on and become curious about sex. Searching for pornography is a way to express this growing interest. Such material is abundant on the Internet and it is easy for children to click on a button that acknowledges that they are 18 and enter some sites (those which do not require a credit card payment). However, such material does not have a captive audience. Hardcore images usually are only accessed by searching for them. If the pornography in question was a billboard at Times Square featuring a lewd display of bestiality involving a woman and a goat, the proponents of the harm to children argument might have a case based on the offensive nature of the image. This would be due to the probability and unavoidable nature of encountering the image. However, this is not the case with the Internet. In order to access these pornographic images, a child must have access to a computer, an account with an Internet service provider, an Internet browser, knowledge of Internet use, often verify that they are over eighteen to enter the site and, sometimes, have a credit card number. While many do have access to such materials, they need not.

A computer does not magically connect itself to the Internet. A parent authorizes the purchase of Internet software and the opening of an account. It is true that this responsibility put on parents may cause some disutility to be incurred for parents who wish to use a computer as an electronic babysitter. This disutility should be factored in when considering regulation. However, there are software packages available that parents can utilize at their discretion which screen out potentially pornographic sites.[37] Also, it should be noted that obtaining an account with an Internet service provider is buying a service and bringing it into one's home, knowing the risks involved. In other words, this is a voluntary association. When a voluntary association is entered into, the contractors accept the risks involved in that association. If parents believe their children are at risk, they may elect not to enter into the association.

An objection which could be made at this point is that Internet spam[38] is not received voluntarily and is quite different from previously considered materials. In many ways, this objection is reasonable. If it were the case that children could be harmed by pornographic images, spam would be quite a problem. However, there are a few points to note here. First, spam may be objectionable for reasons apart from any potential harm involved. Spam is reasonably an invasion of privacy and an annoyance; however, it remains to be considered if such images have harmful effects on children. In addition, although spam is an invasion of sorts, it still remains the case that acquiring an e-mail account is a voluntary association. One of the known risks of having such an account (especially one offered by a free account service) is receiving spam. Again, if one is unwilling to accept the risks in such an association, one should not enter into it. Fortunately, many accounts offer filters that reduce the number of such messages received, and there are strategies to use, such as never giving out one's address online, that help reduce such annoyances. Therefore, if parents do not wish for their children to be bombarded by spam, there are alternatives available.

Proponents of the harm to children argument claim that merely using parental control to regulate access to such materials is not enough to protect children. Howard Poole writes:

> Any method of prevention which does not block the accessibility of pornography must rely on bribes, threats, or coercion which not only require an Argus-eyed supervision but are also likely to stimulate unwanted curiosity in the forbidden subject matter. The only theoretically perfect method of prevention is to rule out logically the possibility of exposure to pornography. Hardly anyone would favor putting out

children's eyes in order to stop them looking at rude books, so the remaining acceptable option lies in making those materials inaccessible through censorship.[39]

However, this dramatic stance simply assumes that the impossibility of access is the best outcome and that such materials are harmful.

Pornography as the Cause of Deviance and Psychological Instability?

Even if children do access pornography and obscenity, the access does not, according to current research, appear to be harmful.[40] That is, children who view pornography are not traumatized and do not grow up to be sex offenders, sex addicts, disturbed criminal deviants or suffer emotional trauma. In *Anatomy of Censorship: Why the Censors Have it Wrong*, Harry White cites many convincing studies and current research which have unanimously concluded that pornography, obscenity, or other objectionable expression do not affect children in any long-term, measurable way. Given all the research currently available, White concludes that "the evidence that obscene material is not harmful is solid," and "there is, today, no reason to question the evidence other than the fact that some people simply don't like the conclusion."[41] Perhaps what is really at issue here is, as Jerry Everard writes, "a popular Disney-like mythology of childhood innocence."[42]

One common fear, as previously mentioned is that if exposed to pornography, children will become sexual offenders or criminal deviants. However, clinicians that specialize in the treatment of sexual offenders do not support this fear. One such clinician, Ray Anderson, writes, "I have specialized in the treatment and assessment of sexual offenders for over thirty years and have been impressed by how infrequently the issue of pornography arises in the treatment or assessment sessions of these patients."[43] In addition to the opinions of clinicians, many studies have been conducted on this subject. To date, the most extensive attempt to study the effects of viewing pornography was the Presidential Commission on Obscenity and Pornography, which issued a multi-volume report, published by the Government Printing Office in 1970. It is worth noting that this study was originally funded using the hypothesis that pornography is harmful to children and women.[44] The Presidential Commission on Obscenity and Pornography condensed the findings of their report in the following statement: "[I]n sum, empirical research, designed to clarify the question, has found no evidence to date that exposure to explicit sexual materials plays a significant role in the causation of delinquent or criminal behavior among youth or adults, ... sexual or nonsexual deviancy or severe emotional disturbances."[45]

Not surprisingly, when the preliminary draft of the presidential commission's report was presented and found to contain evidence that contradicted the original hypothesis (and what many congressmen had expected), many politicians renounced the report. This eventually paved the trail to the infamous Meese Commission report which, unlike the 1970 report, consisted mostly of the opinions of anti-porn activists and offered little scientific data.[46] However, even this report, using the little scientific evidence that was gathered, concluded that violent films (slasher films) are more likely to promote antisocial behavior than "adults only" pornography.[47]

Notable studies that reach the conclusion that pornography does not harm children by increasing the likelihood that they will become sexual deviants and/or offenders are numerous. Published in the *Journal of Interpersonal Violence*, one study examined 82 juvenile sexual offenders ages 9–18 and found that there were significant differences between the offenders and a control group composed of juveniles who were not offenders. Self-report and record data were gathered on family history, education, behavior problems, criminal history, history of abuse and exposure to pornography. Offenders had higher instances of family abuse and violence; however, there was not a difference between offenders and the control group in regard to exposure to pornography. This included age at which exposure occurred and amount of exposure the youths had.[48]

Another study gathered data from adult sexual offenders and controls and also found that early exposure to pornography in childhood did not differ between the two groups. While this study did rely on self-reported data, it has been replicated many times with the same result.[49] Still again, another study analyzed data reported by a large group of sexual offenders, criminal offenders and controls. Like the previously mentioned study, the conclusion was that there is not a correlation between pornography exposure in childhood and criminal deviance. This study examined the frequency of use of pornography, age of exposure to pornography, age of first masturbation and use of pornography during masturbation.[50] None of these factors proved to be significant. In fact, a greater percentage of the control group had been exposed to pornography as children than the group of offenders.[51] In short, the studies support the claim made by Dr. William Stayton of the University of Pennsylvania when he testified in *Reno v. ACLU* that explicit sexual information including pornography does not cause harm to minors of any age. This, Stayton claimed, is also the mainstream view among sex educators and psychologists who specialize in this area.[52]

Of course, to only detail the studies that support my claims against the harm to children argument would be hopelessly biased. There have, in fact, been laboratory studies which suggest that exposure to violent pornography, in the short term,[53] increases aggressiveness and makes participants more accepting of violence towards women.[54] These results are especially worrisome because children often imitate the aggressive models they see growing up. Support of this can be seen in the numerous studies that lead to the conclusion that children who are spanked and beaten often rely on aggressive models to deal with problems.[55] Thus, if children are exposed to violent pornography it is possible that they will repeat the violent behavior they witness in the pornography.

While studies suggesting an increase in aggression after viewing violent pornography are disturbing, there is little evidence to suggest that the sexually explicit content in violent pornography is correlated to aggression at all. In fact, in several studies where violent movies, such as *The Texas Chainsaw Massacre*, were shown, subjects also reported a temporary increase in aggression and negative attitudes concerning women.[56] In fact, there have been studies that conclude that children who, in the absence of contrasting information, view an abundance of media violence tend to be violent (at least temporarily).[57]

While the evidence is weak at best and contradicted by many other studies, an advocate of the regulation of sexually explicit Internet materials may view the previously mentioned evidence as reason to regulate not only pornography, but also, all violence. However, children cannot be encased in a shell and protected from all violence in the world. In fact, making violence or sex taboo may be the worst thing a parent can do. Evidence suggests that the best way to stop any increase, even a temporary increase, in aggression or negative sexual attitudes, is to make sex less taboo and more open. Psychologists Wayne Weiten and Margaret Lloyd write, "ultimately, parents who make sex a taboo topic, end up reducing their influence on their kids' evolving sexual identity. Their children turn elsewhere to seek information about sexuality. Thus the conspiracy of silence about sex in the home often backfires."[58] In fact, there has been research that suggests that persons who are educated about non-violence and positive attitudes concerning women do not respond violently to violent pornography.[59] Thus, this is a case where it is better to be more open than less.

Another fear is that exposure to pornography in childhood will lead to sexual addiction. The thought of children becoming sexual addicts is frightening to parents. Websites such as www.Software4Parents.com try to alleviate this concern by offering software to "prevent sexual addiction."[60] Even with this software, if sexually explicit Internet material were regulated and minors did not have easy access to such materials, the risk of sexual addiction would be lessened, proponents of regulation claim. However, I believe this claim is much too simplistic and not supported by the evidence.

Websites on sexual addiction abound on the Internet and sites such as www.relife.org offer information on sex, love and food addiction as well as the more common addictions relating to alcohol and drug use. Also, organizations such as Sex and Love Addicts Anonymous and S-Anon have formed to offer support for addicts and their families. However, the concept of sexual addiction itself is dubious. There is no mention of sexual addiction in the fourth edition of the *Diagnostic and Statistical Manual of Mental Disorders* (DSM-IV-TR) and many clinicians do not accept sexual addiction as a disease.

Many people pursue certain ends at a cost to other aspects of their lives. One example may be a painter who cannot stop painting until she is satisfied with the result. However, I have not found any information on painting addiction. One reason could be because this activity is socially approved of. In fact, a painter is more properly thought to be driven, dedicated or brilliant rather than addicted. However, this is not the case with sexual addiction and what was once considered merely weakness of will is now called an addiction.

Even if sexual addiction is a real phenomenon, there is little reason to suspect that childhood exposure to sexually explicit Internet materials is a major cause of such addiction. Children have been viewing sexually explicit material long before the invention of the Internet. As children become aware of themselves as sexed beings they become curious about the body of the opposite sex and sexual relations. I remember sneaking looks in a medical book which contained nude figures and looking at my friend's rather massive collection of *National Geographic* magazines to compare our developing chests with those of the women of many African tribes. After some time, I viewed *Playboy* and visited the house of a friend who had managed to acquire a *Hustler* at a flea market. While the Internet may make access to these materials easier, there has always been access to them. Moreover, claiming that pornography causes an addiction is too simple an explanation.

Virtually any significant behavior has many determinants and any single explanation is probably an oversimplification. The fact is that many people have viewed sexually explicit materials on the Internet and have not become sexual addicts just as most persons have ingested food and experienced love without becoming addicted. To regulate food or love on the basis that it will lead to food addiction or love addiction is clearly ridiculous.

One particularly impressive experiment described in the Presidential Commission on Obscenity and Pornography reported that repeated exposure to pornography caused a decrease in interest. This certainly does not support a hypothesis that pornography causes sex addiction. Also, Parry Aftab in her previously mentioned work, *The Parent's Guide to Protecting Your Children in Cyberspace*, has echoed this sentiment. While Aftab expresses many concerns, he acknowledges that most children seem to get bored after repeated exposure to pornography.[61]

Another possible harm to children caused by sexually explicit

Internet materials could come indirectly. In other words, it could be the case that an increase in pornography leads to more sexual offenses against children by influencing sexual deviants. This is similar to a claim made in the Meese Commission Report[62] and could be another way that easy Internet access to pornography is harmful to children. However, evidence does not support this hypothesis. An extensive study published in *Behavioral Sciences and the Law* examined case histories of sexual offenders and found that very few needed pornography as a stimulant.[63] Another study from the *Journal of Social Issues* examined statistics surrounding the relationship between pornography and sex offences in Denmark. On the basis of various investigations, including a survey of public attitudes and studies of police records, it was established that, at least in the case of child molestation, the increase of available pornography represented a real reduction in the number of sexual offenses against children.[64] Even a review of the research literature by D.D. Knudesen in the conservative *Journal of Family Violence* concludes that there is not a relationship between child sexual abuse and pornography.[65]

Unsatisfactory Evidence and Last Attempts

Given the difficulties in establishing a case for the harm to children argument, many courts are simply throwing out the requirement that harm must be proven in order for regulation to occur. In *Regina v. Butler,* the Supreme Court of Canada concluded that to outlaw pornography "does not demand actual proof of harm." In the appeal to the case of *U.S. v. Playboy Entertainment Group*[66] the Justice Department made a similar statement. They claimed that concerns about youthful "exposure to such materials by minors are based on commonly held moral views about the upbringing of children" and do not require empirical proof.[67] Given this disregard for evidence, Harry White suggests, "when it comes to censorship, facts constitute a nuisance that needs to be ignored."[68] However, other proponents rely on a few isolated cases to try to establish, even against an abundance of evidence, that objectionable material is harmful to children. However, by using isolated cases as "proof," a causal connection cannot be established.

These isolated cases are exposed as unsatisfactory evidence of causation when we look at other isolated cases in history. For example, mass murderer and rapist Heinrich Pomerenke committed his first murder after viewing the film *The Ten Commandments*. He believed the film advocated the argument that women were evil. A murderer who sucked his victims' blood through straws, John George Haigh, was inspired to this activity after watching the Anglican High Church Communion Service.[69] Even with these isolated instances, an argument to the effect that Communion or watching religious films causes homicidal tendencies is simply ridiculous. What a person takes away from these activities depends more on the person than the activities. Given the lack of proof of harm, there is no incentive to believe that pornography or obscenity is not also of this type. Thus, to be consistent, one who wishes to censor the Internet because of this objectionable and "harmful material" would have to wish to censor *The Ten Commandments* and church Communion services because they have inspired a few isolated persons to produce harm.

At this point an objection could be made that the conclusion to the previous paragraph does not follow. It could be maintained that the proponent's arguments that pornography tends to inspire bad behavior is much stronger than the cases I listed involving isolated examples. However, for this objection to hold, proponents must prove that such a trend does exist and show a substantial statistical correlation. This they have not been able to do. Also, consider the case of Heinrich Pomerenke. The Pomerenke case could be seen as just part of a larger claim that watching movies tends to inspire violence. To support this claim, it would not be difficult to find other cases where movies have inspired violent behavior. Furthermore, there are many examples that could suggest harm to minors. For example one case involved four teenagers who raped a 9-year-old girl after watching the movie *Born Innocent* on television.[70] Many individual cases could be cited and it could be claimed that television movies tend to inspire violence but, without a statistical correlation, this claim is ungrounded. Almost any information including books, paintings, television, pictures and others can inspire some people to perform certain actions. However, without a causal connection in place, the actions performed say more about the performer than the material that was inspirational.

Proponents of the harm to children argument are also very selective in which material they wish to regulate. This makes it questionable if harm is the issue at all. For example, while there is a push to censor pornography, sites focusing on violent sports, crime, and cosmetic surgery would remain untouched by most legislation. By age eighteen the average American child has seen over 200,000 violent acts, of which 40,000 are homicides, on television, a censored medium. However, on the same commercial television stations where they are subjected to violence, they cannot view exposed breasts.[71] Also, there is not a call to censor information because it promotes dishonesty or cowardice, although having these traits could be harmful to minors. This reinforces the premise that proponents of the harm to children argument care less about harm than the social enforcement of morality.[72] Also, it is possible that proposed regulation will backfire terribly.

Given the curious nature of children it is possible that regulatory laws may even spark interest in such material like warning labels on music have been noted to do. By making sex and sexually explicit materials taboo, more interest in sex could be created. Perhaps, as illustrated in the story of Adam and Eve, it is human nature to want what is forbidden. When this aspect of human nature is combined with a child's curiosity, this possible consequence of regulation is only amplified. However, even if such regulation does not increase interest in such materials, it also does not, as previously argued, prevent harm from occurring.

In this chapter I have discussed the harm to children argument used by proponents of the regulation of sexually explicit Internet materials. It should be clear that this argument cannot justify regulation of such materials. The fears that proponents of this argument express are unwarranted and certainly not strong enough to justify regulation. In fact, it is possible that more harm will come to children if sexually explicit materials are regulated than if they are made taboo.

5

Harm to Women

Introduction

A common argument for the regulation of pornography and obscenity on the Internet, while far from Internet specific, claims that pornographic materials cause harm to women. Given that an abundance of pornographic materials exists on the Internet, it is feasible to conclude, using this argument, that an unregulated Internet is harmful to women. Throughout much of history women have been subjugated, demeaned and considered less than persons. If pornography causes these attitudes and contributes to or causes harm to women, it is as abhorrent as past atrocities and surely a sound reason for blocking the easy access afforded by the Internet. In this chapter I will examine the question of whether easy access to pornographic materials is, in fact, harmful to women.

A Feminist Definition of Pornography?

Feminist writers cannot agree on what exactly constitutes pornography; however, many agree that it is harmful to women. Some writers define pornography as that which degrades and demeans the human female.[1] The famous (or infamous) antipornography legislation which Catharine MacKinnon, a professor of law at the University of Michigan, spearheaded, defined pornography as "the graphic sexually explicit subordination[2] of women, whether in pictures or words." To be pornographic, according to this definition, the subordinating material must also include one of the following:

1. Women are presented as dehumanized sexual objects, things or commodities,

2. Women are presented as sexual objects who enjoy humiliation or pain,

3. Women are presented as sexual objects experiencing sexual pleasure in rape, incest, or other sexual assault,

4. Women are presented as sexual objects tied up or cut up or mutilated or bruised or physically hurt,

5. Women are presented as being penetrated by objects or animals,

6. Women are presented in postures or positions of sexual submission or display,

7. Women's body parts — including but not limited to vaginas, breasts or buttocks — are exhibited such that women are reduced to those parts,

8. Women are presented in scenarios of degradation, humiliation, injury, torture, shown as filthy or inferior, bleeding, bruised or hurt in a context that makes these conditions sexual.[3]

While this definition is extensive it is also vague and likely to capture things that are not, by most standards, pornographic. An example is Roman Polanski's classic film *Repulsion*. In the film, a woman is shown being forced to engage in sexual intercourse and even enjoying rape.[4] She is put into an inferior position, subordinated and used merely for enjoyment in one section of the film. However, to regulate this film and label it pornographic due to one scene would ignore the great artistic value of the work. In fact, many works of art, including nude paintings, focus on women's body parts and, according to this definition would be pornographic. In short, this definition allows a work to be labeled without considering the broader content or artistic merit of the piece. As Catherine MacKinnon writes, "if a woman is subjugated, why should it matter that the work has other value?"[5]

To help in the quest to establish a definition, many feminist writers have tried to differentiate between pornography and erotica.[6] Often associated with pornography and not erotica is pornography's tendency to objectify women and reduce them to body parts. In *Letters From a*

War Zone Andrea Dworkin writes of this tendency in pornography. She claims that in pornography "women's body parts are exhibited such that women are reduced to those parts."[7] However, this definition also fails to consider works in a broader context. If we were to label all works that reduce females to body parts or portray close-ups of sexual organs, many classic paintings such as Matisse's *Blue Nude* and some feminist art[8] would be labeled pornographic.[9]

Despite the aforementioned difficulties, many feminists have persisted in advocating a broad definition of pornography. For example, Andrea Dworkin includes all sexual depictions[10] in her definition of pornography. In this definition Dworkin never spells out exactly what a sexual depiction is and often writes in circularities.[11] However, she points out that "pornography" is derived from the Greek words *porne* (whore) and *graphos* (writing) and concludes that pornography is "writing about whores." From this she claims that all such depictions of women that show them in a sexual fashion are harmful[12] to women.[13] Of this "writing about whores" she maintains, "the only change in the meaning of the word is with respect to the second part, *graphos*: now there are cameras — there is still photography, film, video."[14] While the definitions vary, what is clear, however, to antipornography feminists is that whatever pornography is, it should be banned. As Andrea Dworkin writes, "protecting what they say is protecting what they do to us."[15] In fact, Catharine MacKinnon goes so far as to claim that pornography is sexual abuse and should be regulated in the same fashion as all sexual abuse.[16] Although definitional ambiguities remain, and an agreed upon definition is unlikely to be formulated, in the following section I will examine the reasons given by some feminist writers as to why pornography is harmful to women and should be regulated.

Supporting premises for the conclusion that pornography is harmful to women are numerous. One that is often stated is that pornography harms the women involved in its production.[17] It has also been claimed that pornography is correlated with violent crimes against women. However, perhaps the best articulated feminist claims are that pornography causes negative attitudes about women which contributes to social inequality, often to the point of depriving them of their positive liberties and that pornography defames and is libelous to women.

Harm and the Production of Pornography

Andrea Dworkin and others have argued that the models who perform in pornographic works are treated as mere means by the consumers (and often the producers) of pornography. Worse still, it is often claimed that women working in the sex industry are both physically and mentally abused. To support these assertions, Dworkin relies on a series of case studies, including the story of Linda Lovelace.[18] Catherine MacKinnon also mentions Lovelace as "evidence" of such abuse being widespread.[19] While it is true that many people use pornography merely as a means of obtaining pleasure, this does not lead to the conclusion that the women who are featured in pornography are treated *merely* as means. The models or performers in adult entertainment may be perfectly happy to be featured in such materials in exchange for monetary compensation. The same can be said of most service industries. When a taxi driver is giving me a lift, I am only interested in him or her for the service he or she is providing me. I pay him or her and walk away after the cab arrives at its destination. I do not care who he or she is or what he or she feels. I just want to use the service to obtain my goal. I do not deceive him or her in any way and, perhaps, through my payment, do not use him or her merely as a means. The models and performers in the sex industry are also paid and informed as to what their services will be used for. While it is true that consumers may not want to know the models or performers as persons, this is no worse than a ride in a taxicab. To claim that these models cannot autonomously[20] agree to engage in such work is to portray them as easily misguided and unable to consent. Many models and actresses in sexually explicit productions affirm their choice of careers and refute the idea that they are abused and/or unable to consent. Nina Hartley, an actress in pornographic films, claims that the sex industry "provides a surprisingly flexible and supportive arena for me to grow as a performer, both sexually and nonsexually." Of her career she also claims that "an intelligent, sexual women could choose a job in the sex industry and not be a victim, but instead emerge even stronger and more self-confident, with a feeling, even, of self-actualization."[21] Hartley is far from alone in her assertion that being part of the pornography industry is an autonomous choice.

Many actresses in pornographic films have come forward and articulated positions similar to Hartley. Two of the best known actresses to express such a position are Candida Royalle, who is now the president of Femme Productions, and Gloria Leonard. Both women claim that acting in pornographic films was an autonomous choice and are frequent speakers and writers for organizations such as Feminists for Free Expression.[22]

As for the claim that models and performers are physically abused in the production of pornography, even some feminist writers who argue against pornography admit that, even in "victim pornography,"[23] the models used in its production are not necessarily harmed.[24] While it may be the fact that physical harm is portrayed, there is no reason why pornographic materials cannot be produced without harming the models and/or performers. In fact, many pornography distributors, such as Femme Productions[25] and Blush Productions,[26] are working towards improved working conditions for their actors.[27] Candida Royalle of Femme Productions even advocates the formation of a sex workers union to insure that models and performers are afforded safe and comfortable working environments.[28]

For any product and/or service there is bound to be a producer or distributor who mistreats their workers. One area where this is evident is on farms where migrant workers are employed and live in shacks without electricity or running water.[29] However, just because there are these cases, the conclusion that farm production or migrant labor, in general, should not be practiced does not follow. Working as a pornography actor or model is a voluntary association and, while undesirable working conditions may provide an argument for unionization or labor regulations, they do not support disallowing this association.[30] Restriction may, actually, contribute to worse working conditions. If such productions were driven underground, it would be nearly impossible for models and performers to seek legal protections against violence and duress in the workplace.

Pornography and Sexual Violence

A common argument for restricting the availability of pornography centers on the claim that men tend to commit violent acts against women after viewing pornography. This argument has a long history and has been reformulated many times. J. Edgar Hoover is quoted as saying, "the increase in the number of sex crimes is due precisely to sex literature madly presented in certain magazines. Filthy literature is the great moral wrecker. It is creating criminals faster than jails can be built."[31] A formulation of this argument was behind the attempt of the United States Congress to pass the Pornography Victims Compensation Act (PVCA) in 1992. This act, popularly called the "Bundy Bill," was spurred by convicted rapist and murderer Ted Bundy's claim that exposure to pornography caused him to commit violent sex crimes. The PVCA proposed that victims of sexual crimes be allowed to seek monetary damages from pornography distributors based on the belief that pornography is a causal factor in some sexual assaults.[32]

As common as the claim that pornography causes sexual violence is, there is no solid supportive statistical evidence showing a correlation[33] between pornography and sexual violence.[34] While stories of sex offenders being pornography addicts are often cited, this does little to prove causation. As in the case of arguments claiming harm to children, what one receives from such material often depends more on the person than the material. As Barbara Dority points out, Charles Manson claims to have been inspired by the Bible and John Hinkley testified that he knew he had to kill former president of the United States Ronald Reagan after reading *Catcher in the Rye*. Of course, while the number of persons claiming to have been inspired by pornography to commit violent acts is surely more than two, it does not appear to amount to a significant correlation.

Several studies have examined the role of pornography in sexual offense. One study interviewed 227 sexual offenders and a control group about their purchases of pornography. After the data was compiled, the statistics failed to show a link between the use of violent pornography and sexual offense.[35] Another study focused on the relationship between pornography and rape. This study gathered data from the Uniform Crime Reports and circulation data from pornographic magazines. Using Standard Metropolitan Statistical Areas as units of analysis, a correlation between pornography and rape was not supported. In fact, although population size, the proportion of young adults, the divorce rate and population change were all significant variables, the circulation rate of pornography did not correlate with sexual offense.

The claim that sexually explicit material causes the negative attitudes and aggressive tendencies that contribute to sexual offense has also been studied extensively. In controlled laboratory experiments, many studies have been conducted that conclude that sexually explicit material does not produce aggression towards women. One such study, reported in the *Journal of Sex Research*, sought to test the hypothesis that exposure to pornography would cause men to exhibit negative attitudes concerning women. This study is particularly interesting because it does not rely on self-reported data. In the study, subjects watched a violent pornographic video and then were provoked by a female experimenter who treated them harshly. Subjects could respond to this behavior in non-aggressive or aggressive ways (including the use of electric shock). Contrary to the original hypothesis used in the study, there was little difference between the behavior of the subjects and controls who were not exposed to the video.[36]

Field studies have also concluded that there is not a link between exposure to pornography and negative or aggressive attitudes towards women. A particularly interesting study randomly assigned groups of men to either watch pornography four hours each day over five days or watch introduction to psychology films. Using surveys administered both before and after the exposure period, data collected failed to show a difference in attitudes concerning women between the control and experimental group.[37]

Even if a correlation could be shown between pornography possession and sexual crimes, it would be insufficient to prove causation. It may be the case that those who commit sexual crimes are attracted to pornography, not that pornography causes sexual crimes. Faulty relationships of this sort often emerge in claims of correlation. A humorous example of such a claim of correlation involves the hair conditioner Pantene. The company that manufactures Pantene conducted a survey and "found" that 51% of women who use conditioner daily enjoy active sex lives. This is compared to only 31% of those who are not conditioner users. Given this correlation, the company sought to put forth the "fact" that conditioner can make one's sex live more active.[38] Clearly this conclusion is absurd as it ignores many extraneous variables. Even if the study was replicable and relied on sound data, it could be the case that conditioner just happens to appeal to persons who have active sex lives. In fact, this is likely as more persons between the ages of 20 and 60 use conditioner more often than those who are older or younger. Also, it could be the case that those who put more effort into their appearance have active sex lives. While I know of no studies that support either of the previous two hypotheses, I am merely pointing to the absurdity of drawing a conclusion based merely on what is likely to be an incidental correlation.

Also, if exposure to pornography is a major cause of sexual violence, there would be difficulties in explaining the fact that in parts of Eastern Europe and the Middle East where there is relatively little pornography, there is a great deal of sexual violence. On the other hand, in the Netherlands and Scandinavia, where there are few restrictions on pornography, the rate of sex-related crime is lower than in the United States.[39] Aryeh Neier writes, "[F]or example, violence against women is common in ... Ireland and South Africa, but pornography is unavailable in those countries. By contrast violence against women is relatively uncommon in Denmark, Sweden and the Netherlands, although pornography seems to be even more plentifully available than in the United States."[40] Many studies have been conducted that support this conclusion.[41] While there may be other causes of the violence in countries without such exposure to pornography, if pornography were a major causal factor in sexual violence we would expect more sexual violence in countries where pornography is most abundant.

Japan provides yet another example to consider. From 1972 to 1995 the availability of pornography in Japan increased notably while the incidence of rape and other sexual assaults decreased substantially.[42] This is especially notable as Japan has, perhaps, the most sadistic pornography in the world. Pornography in Japan often features simulated rape and cruelty to females. Ian Buruma has claimed that pornography in Japan may have cathartic effects. He writes that pornographic violence, "in Japan as elsewhere, is a way of relieving fear, of exorcizing the demons."[43]

In fact, many studies suggest that the availability of pornography is actually correlated with positive attitudes concerning women and a decrease in sexual crimes. One study gathered data concerning the circulation rates of pornographic magazines and gender equality in the United States. Gender equality was measured in this study using the Gender Equality Index (GEX). Using this data, multiple regression analysis was used to test the hypothesis that higher circulation rates would positively correlate with lower levels of gender equality. However, contrary to the original hypothesis, the study found that states with higher circulation rates had higher gender equality scores.[44] Another study examined the attitudes of college men and women (who did not regularly visit adult theaters) and patrons of adult theaters. Through an interview and survey process, this study gathered evidence that the patrons of adult theaters actually had more favorable attitudes towards women than the control subjects.[45]

In sharp contrast to a relationship between pornography and sexual violence, many studies have been conducted that point to the possible cathartic effects of pornography. One such study concluded that many sexual offenders have used pornography to relieve the impulse to commit a sexual offence.[46] This is given further support by cross-cultural studies. Many studies examining data before and after the Danish liberation of pornography laws have concluded that the higher the availability of pornography, the fewer sexual crimes are committed in Denmark.[47] While this could be the result of attitude changes or cathartic effects, the evidence is strong enough to support the conclusion that the availability of pornography certainly does not *increase* the occurrence of sexual crimes. In fact, the overwhelming evidence that pornography does not cause violence has forced many authors to make bold statements to this effect. Jonathan Rauch writes, "No respectable study or evidence has shown any causal link between pornography and actual violence."[48]

Pornography and Incitement

While a causal connection is not forthcoming, there may still be cause to believe that pornography can contribute to sexual violence by inciting perpetrators of sexual crimes. This contribution to harm would differ little from those made by human accomplices to crime. For example, suppose that Smith commits a rape that he would not have committed but for information communicated to him by Jones. Can Jones be held partly accountable for the rape? In some circumstances he can. If the information that Jones gave Smith was intended to help Smith commit the rape, Jones could incur liability. However, Jones may also incur liability if the information were an encouragement or assumed a position of advocacy.

While pornography does not fit this advocacy model exactly, it is possible that it could be an incitement to violence. Inciting a crime can incur liability and, as pointed to in Mill's famous corn dealer example, may be a causal factor in a crime. While haranguing an angry crowd on the doorstep of a corn dealer may incite mob violence, the same act performed several hours prior would have no effect. The same may be true of pornography: it could endorse rape and other forms of violence against women when presented to an already susceptible[49] public. As Catherine MacKinnon writes of pornography, "the message of these materials, and there is one, as there is to all conscious activity, is 'get her.' Pointing at all women."[50] However, it is dubious to claim that pornography encourages or endorses rape or other forms of sexual assault.

While some pornography may portray violence against women, it is quite possible to portray something without endorsing it. To claim that pornography endorses violence is similar to claiming that newspapers endorse crimes simply because they depict them. Even depictions that are intended to endorse something may fail at doing so. Consider the old and infamous documentary film *Reefer Madness* that was intended to endorse the view that smoking marijuana would be a catalyst to the destruction of society. Today audiences laugh at the depiction, which fails at persuading. Furthermore, it is not agreed upon as to what, exactly, pornography is supposed to be expressing. It has even been argued that pornography libels men and endorses the view that they are sex hungry beasts; however, there is little concern given to regulating it on this account.[51] The fact of the matter is that many men who never have and never will commit violent acts against women view pornography. For the majority of these persons, it never serves as an endorsement or incitement.

Speech as Sex and Sex as Speech

Given the failure to prove pornography causes or incites violence, many feminist writers have sought other routes to demonstrate that pornography is harmful in and of itself. In the extreme, this claim is made by Catharine MacKinnon. MacKinnon argues that pornography is a sexual act and constitutes sexual discrimination. In her book, *Only Words*, MacKinnon elaborates on this thesis and writes, "[A]s sex becomes speech, speech becomes sex."[52] She further writes, " [P]ornography is masturbation material. It is used as sex. It therefore is sex."[53] She claims that men "experience this being done by watching it being done" in the form of masturbation.[54] MacKinnon's statements are reminiscent of George Orwell's work *Nineteen Eighty-Four*, where the concept of *thoughtcrime* is discussed. Orwell writes, "in the eyes of the Party, there was no distinction between thought and deed."[55]

MacKinnon defends her position by pointing to the fact that many words are, she claims, "unproblematically treated as acts."[56] Examples she gives include the words "you're fired" and "sleep with me and I'll give you an A." She claims that this speech, like pornography, constitutes a discriminatory act.[57] What she fails to acknowledge, however, is that these words would be meaningless and constitute nothing without the actions that they signify. Thinking about or saying something alone does not amount to doing it. MacKinnon seems to acknowledge this when she writes, "pornography does not leap off the shelf and assault women: men do, men who are made, changed, and impelled by it."[58] She continues, "women could, in theory, walk safely past whole warehouses full of it, quietly resting in its jackets. It is what it takes to make it and what happens through its use that are the problem." In this acknowledgment, MacKinnon appears to be backing away from the idea that pornography is, in and of itself, sexual discrimination; however, it is not long before she is again claiming that pictures of sex *are* sex. At one point, she even admits that she is not certain as to how viewing pornography becomes sex. She writes, "I am not ultimately sure why this is the case, but it has something to do with the positioning of sex words in sexual abuse, in abuse as sex, in sex as abuse, in sex."[59] Given that MacKinnon herself is not certain as to how this transition takes place, her argument for there being such a transition is, at best, weak.

Pornography as Libel

Two claims that women are harmed by pornography that are, on the surface more plausible, involve the content of pornography. The first of these is that pornography libels women. Libel is the legal term for a defamatory statement or representation that conveys an unjustly unfavorable impression. Given that it is illegal to commit libel, it has been argued that pornography should, to be consistent, also be illegal. On this subject, Judith Hill writes:

> The pornography industry regularly publishes material which, speaking conservatively, tends to contribute to the perpetuation of derogatory beliefs about womankind. Victim pornography, in particular, depicts women not simply as ill treated, but as eager to be used and abused, totally lacking in human dignity: as more or less worthless for any purpose other than casual sexual intercourse.[60]

In other words, the pornography industry is lying about women. This, it is argued, constitutes libel. Hill writes, "libel has never been protected by the First Amendment, and it is unlikely that even the most liberal of civil libertarians would be tempted to argue that it should be."[61] Surely libel can be harmful and, if pornography is the cause of such harm to women, there may be a strong case for regulation. However, this claim is dubious.

While it is quite likely that a certain pornographic picture may be degrading to the person (or persons) featured in the picture and depict her (or them) as "eager to be used and abused," this does not necessarily libel *all* women. Many persons in countless works of art are portrayed in a negative light but the artworks are not libelous to any group. For example, it surely would be unreasonable to claim that all fat men are defamed by Shakespeare's portrayal of Falstaff. This unreasonableness even holds true when there is a vast amount of material available that portrays persons with certain characteristics in a negative fashion. For example, it is often the case that in historical depictions of early America, persons with white skin are shown as cruel, violent, greedy and supportive of slavery.[62] While this depiction does portray the historical figures featured in a negative light, it says nothing about all people with white skin. It also cannot be generalized to all persons with white skin who lived in the historical period featured.

Also, the claim that pornography libels women assumes that pornography is propositional; however, this may not be the case. Libel is distinguished, legally, from all false statements by the fact that, in libel, the false statements are required to be defamatory and unjustly convey an unfavorable impression. Pornography does not promulgate falsities about women. In other words, it is not defamatory. Pornography is pure fantasy and creates a dramatic space where things are larger than life and reality is purposefully[63] put aside.[64] Fantasies do not assert anything. Quite the opposite, fantasies are usually an escape from reality. If women were truly sex slaves available to all interested and enjoyed degrading treatment, there likely would not be a market for such fantasy material. While the fantastic nature of expressed fantasy need not be immediately apparent, I believe it is in most pornography. Anyone who lives and interacts with women will readily be able to ascertain that they are not like the characters in pornography. Pornography cannot be false in the way that a statement of fact can be because of this fantasy framework. In fact, it is quite plausible that pornography is not really communication about (and certainly thus not an endorsement of) any view of women.

Pornography is, in many ways, similar to romance novels. Surely if the passages of romance novels were viewed as asserting facts, they would present an extremely distorted view of men. Men in such novels are portrayed as valiant heroes who sweep women off their feet and make love like stallions. Certainly claiming that all men are like this is false and may cause harm by endorsing an impossibly high standard. In one case such material even served as a catalyst for harm.[65] Nannie Doss poisoned four husbands because she believed that none had lived up to the stud-like image portrayed in her *True Romances* novels.[66] In addition romance novels may present a degrading view of men as "nothing but studs." However, if a claim of libel were brought against romance novels it would be preposterous because romance novels are fantasy. Also, it is unreasonable to regulate romance novels because some contain descriptions of some men that are degrading. The differences in the attitudes between libel in romance novels and pornography are hard to explain. Both are fantasies that portray characters of a particular gender as they are not and in a degrading fashion. Perhaps fantasy is only libelous when we disapprove of the fantasy material. This of course brings us back to square one, and we must justify this disapproval. If we try to justify the disapproval by claiming libel, the argument is simply circular. Furthermore, given that this would be a case of group libel, it is not clear that, even if it were libelous, it should be illegal.

Group libel cases are incredibly difficult to judge as there is no one person that can claim to be the victim of such speech. While it is true that in 1952 the United States Supreme Court ruled in *Beauharnais v. Illinois*[67] that libelous utterances, whether directed at individuals or "designated collectives,"[68] are not constitutionally protected, cases after *Beauharnais* have had different results. Also, while this initial ruling focused on political speech, subsequent rulings have encompassed a wide array of speech. In *New York Times v. Sullivan,* group libel was given some constitutional protection. In this case, the Court ruled that "debate on public issues should be uninhibited, robust, and wide-open."[69] Since this ruling the court has constantly ruled not to uphold group libel claims because they may thwart public debate. Therefore, in the United States, persons can claim that Jewish people created the Holocaust to gain sympathy or even march through a Jewish neighborhood proclaiming such sentiments.[70] Thus, even if the highly improbable claim that pornography libels women were true, it is not clear that it should be restricted by current legal standards.

In fact, it could be argued that most pornography (especially hardcore pornography) is not speech at all. In many ways pornography is closer to a sexual aid than a depiction or endorsement. Publishers and producers of pornography do not intend to communicate anything: they only intend to arouse the purchaser. Claiming that pornography is speech is similar to claiming that a vibrator shaped like a human penis is speech that degrades men. In reality, neither says anything about men or women; they merely aid in sexual gratification.

A rebuttal could be made in that if one deconstructs pornography and looks into its "deeper" meaning, an endorsement will be evident. However, I believe that if it is necessary to "deconstruct" something to find its meaning it is probable that an objective meaning is not readily available. In such cases, it is likely that what messages a person receives during a deconstruction is dependent on the meaning he or she was looking for and/or expecting. While such deconstructing may reveal something about the person who deconstructs the pornography and, perhaps, society as a whole, it does support the conclusion that such a "deeper" meaning or endorsement exists. However, even if pornography does not libel women and cannot be restricted under current legal principles it may still subordinate women and cause harm.

Pornography and Equality

Many authors have claimed that pornography degrades women, often to the point of impeding their liberties. This is, as is the previous argument, a sweeping claim in that it includes the whole class of women. In other words, proponents claim that pictures featuring certain women are degrading to all women. Andrea Dworkin often claims that pornography subordinates all women and leads to sex inequality. Moreover, as previously mentioned, it is claimed that, in pornography, negative attitudes concerning women are not only portrayed, they are endorsed. Through this endorsement, it is argued that pornography teaches negative attitudes about women. Helen Longino writes, "[W]hat makes a work a work of pornography, then, is not simply its representation of degrading and abusive sexual encounters, but its implicit, if not explicit, approval and recommendation of sexual behavior that is immoral."[71] Further, it is claimed that by creating such endorsements and a climate where women are viewed as less than equal, their positive liberties could be obstructed.

In a democracy, everyone should be able to participate equally in self-governance and positive liberty should be secured for all. In other words, everyone should have an equal opportunity to make themselves heard. However, if pornography degrades the status of women, it is unclear that their opinions and beliefs will count as much as they should. Ronald Dworkin summarizes this argument, "women cannot have genuine political power or authority because they are perceived and understood unauthentically — that is they are made over by male fantasy into people very different from, and of much less consequence than, the people they really are."[72] The argument claims that because of pornography, women are denied equal positive liberty. Thus, this is a situation where some speech may limit the speech of others. As Rae Langton writes, "[T]he free speech of men silences the free speech of women."[73] Some of the most adamant defenders of this position argue that free speech is what they value most. They claim that pornography is silencing and, therefore, opposed to free speech, not the other way around. Catharine MacKinnon writes, "both pornography and its protection have deprived women of speech, especially speech against sexual abuse."[74] Using this argument, if the Internet is not regulated, free speech is hindered. This argument is especially strong because it appeals to two common liberal principles: equality and liberty. If pornography blocks both equality and positive liberties for a class of persons, it would be illogical for a liberal not to wish that it be regulated.

The claim that pornography is the major cause of degradation which could eventually lead to denial of positive liberties is unconvincing. For this argument to be plausible, it has to be true that pornography is a major cause of negative and derogatory attitudes concerning women. This is exactly the claim that MacKinnon makes when she argues that by portraying male supremacy and domination in pornography, they are made real. If this argument is sound, it leads to the conclusion that pornography (apart from any crimes it might inspire) oppresses and degrades women.

It is paradoxical, however, to claim that pornography is a major cause of negative attitudes given that, in the last fifty years, the production of pornography has grown rapidly while attitudes about women have changed positively.[75] Also, consider the horrible treatment and attitudes towards women that were pervasive in previous centuries when access to pornography was limited. If pornography is not a major cause of these attitudes, there is little support for the argument that pornography causes subordination of women. Also, if pornography does not cause negative attitudes, it does not aid in the denial of liberties.

Sex in Society and the Slippery Slope

Sexual images are just one possible way of creating an environment that is degrading to women. Personally, I believe commercials for cleaning aids in which women are usually depicted in an apron cleaning are more offensive and degrading than most pornography. The same is true of many other vintage television programs, such as *I Dream of Jeannie*. However, I would be hard-pressed to formulate a valid argument that commercials and vintage television programs should be regulated. As Joel Feinberg writes, "[T]here is no doubt that much pornography does portray women in subservient positions, but if that is defamatory to women in anything like the legal sense, then so are soap commercials on TV. So are many novels, even some good ones. That some groups are portrayed in unflattering roles has not hitherto been a ground for the censorship of fiction or advertising."[76] Yes, there are women in pornography that are portrayed in a degrading fashion; however, as previously argued, this certainly does not necessarily endorse negative attitudes about women as a class.

I would be unsuccessful if I tried to argue that commercials and vintage television programs are a major contributor of degrading attitudes about women. Such commercials are appealing and sell a product because of a set of previously existing attitude structures. If they did not have a market to appeal to, they would not sell products. In fact, by concentrating on commercials or pornography as a cause of degradation we might be obscured from finding the real causes of degrading attitudes towards females. At the very least, the specter of as yet unidentified multiple causes for anti-social behavior should put caution in those who isolate blame. The cause of these attitudes about women has been speculated about by Joel Feinberg. Feinberg claims that it is the "cult of macho" that leads to these attitudes. This cult of macho is similar to the machismo attitude that is often found in Spanish cultures. It involves the conception of a man as the power in a family and places an emphasis on manliness, strength and violence. Feinberg writes, "the cult of macho expectations is itself the primary cause of both the existence of violent pornography (it provides the appreciative audience) and of the real-life sexual violence (it provides the motive)."[77]

Besides the current social structure and the "cult of the macho" there have emerged many other candidates for the cause of negative attitudes towards women. Carole Pateman regards the marriage contract as the foundation of all gender inequality.[78] With these competing candidates, and no statistical evidence[79] to support the position that pornography causes derogatory attitudes and subordination, there is little support for the claim of harm to women. In fact, as I will discuss in Chapter Seven, pornography may, actually, have great value for women. Pornography breaks the mold of current acceptable attitudes and can be potentially freeing against the cult of the macho. As Stanford law professor Kathleen Sullivan writes:

> [I]f social convention, backed by religion and law, confines sexuality to the heterosexual monogamous, marital familial, and reproductive, the ambisexual, promiscuous, adulterous, selfish, and gratification-centered world of pornography is a charter of sexual revolution that is potentially liberating rather than confining for women.[80]

In this chapter, I have examined the claim that sexually explicit Internet materials should be regulated because pornography is harmful to women. Not only is the claim unsupported and unsound, acceptance of it can be dangerous. Accepting this claim to harm would be the beginning of a very slippery slope. In general, many slippery slope arguments tend to be faulted because they do not give a substantive reason why protections would not be effective and/or why sliding down the slope is probable. However, in this case, many pressures exist to slide down the slope. If the harm to women argument were accepted, to be consistent, racist literature and any other speech that any group believes portrays them in a negative manner would be subject to regulation. In fact, we may already be a good distance down this slope. This is problematic as many classics portray a time when Native Americans and African Americans were seen and portrayed as less than full persons. If pornography and/or hate speech is truly harmful, it will not be less harmful simply because the piece depicting it is a masterpiece. Regulating such great works would be unfortunate indeed.

6

Harm to the Moral Environment and Offense

Introduction

A great deal of the sexually explicit material on the Internet is offensive to many people. Perhaps some of this offense is due to the fact that pornography is widely considered to be immoral. Because of its offensive nature and perceived immorality, some authors have claimed that pornography harms the moral environment[1] and/or is intolerably offensive and should be regulated. In fact, it has been argued that the widespread availability of such materials, like that offered on the Internet, is harmful to society's moral fabric and may cause a horribly offensive environment. That is, one offensive and/or immoral act or thing, in and of itself, may not be harmful; however, many offensive actions and/or materials together could cause a harmful disintegration of the communal environment in a society. If this claim can be substantiated, it is possible that Internet regulation of sexually explicit material may be justifiable.

Examples of the claim that offensive materials can cause harm to the moral environment are numerous. In his book *Slouching Towards Gomorrah: Modern Liberalism and American Decline*,[2] Robert Bork argues that we are sliding into immorality fueled by uncensored Internet pornography and obscenity.[3] Bork writes: "[A]merican popular culture is in a free fall, with the bottom yet in sight."[4] Tim Lahaye calls pornography that exists on the Internet a "mental poison" and claims that it corrupts teens and destroys families.[5] In his article "America's Slide into the Sewer," George Will blames recent violent acts and the "slide into the sewer" on musical lyrics and pornography. Will also believes that pornography is largely responsible for current moral decay.[6] Examples of similar arguments are numerous and usually center around the claims that access to pornography may create a type of offensive "cultural pollution" and that pornography contributes to an increase of immoral ideas and behaviors. Given that the Internet provides easy access to sexually explicit materials, those who fear that pornography is harmful to society often claim that an unregulated Internet is fuel for this harmful fire of immorality and extreme offense. In what follows I will examine the claims that pornography on the Internet could lead to a harmful moral slippage and that Internet pornography should be regulated because it may harm communities in the form of moral pollution and unendurable offense.

Background

Sexually explicit materials and even nudity itself have a history of being targeted as offensive, immoral and the cause of moral decline. In this section I will briefly trace the history and effects of these beliefs. This will be done in an effort to better understand the current claims formulated against sexually explicit Internet materials. Once brought forth, it is clear that historical patterns exist regarding sexually explicit materials that are being reinvented today.

As an example of the resurgence of historical patterns consider the once booming industry that existed in Europe which centered around painting over uncovered penises in works of art and attaching fig leaves to sculptures.[7] This theme is carried on today in the Untied States where the Department of Justice spent eight thousand dollars on blue velvet drapes to cover a giant statue. The statue, *The Spirit of Justice*, represents justice and is a woman with arms raised and a toga covering all but a single breast.[8]

Formal ordinances and regulation against sexually explicit materials can also be seen throughout history. Like many current arguments, the justification for such ordinances was often the protection of the moral environment. In 1857, the lord chief justice of England introduced the Obscene Publications Act into the House of Lords in an effort to censor sexually explicit materials. The lord chief justice claimed of the bill that it would eliminate the "sale of poison more deadly than prussic acid, strychnine or arsenic." He claimed that this "poison would corrupt the morals of children,"[9] women, the "weak of mind" and be harmful to society.[10] Concern for moral slippage and cultural pollution in communities continues to be reflected in recent proposals to regulate sexually explicit Internet materials. In 1998[11] Michael Oxley, in a hearing to address legislative proposals to regulate the Internet, claimed that a recent national poll found that the top concern of voters in the United States was the moral decline of society.[12] To address this concern, Oxley supports the regulation of sexually explicit Internet materials.

In addition to governmental legislation, many organizations have been formed throughout history to fight potential moral decline. For example, protection from harm to the moral environment was the reason given for the formation of the Legion of Decency. The Legion of Decency was an organization formed by the American bishops of the Roman Catholic Church in 1936. The legion's purpose was to rate films and identify films with morally objectionable content. The legion developed a list of recommended and non-recommended films (essentially banned films) and distributed the list to members of the Catholic Church and the general public. The legion had a powerful influence in the 1930s and 1940s, and many American citizens took a pledge promising never to attend any morally objectionable movie or frequent any theater that would show an objectionable movie. The legion's ratings were very strict; even *Miracle on 34th Street* was rated morally objectionable in part because it featured a divorced woman.[13] Even with the strict ratings, the legion was very effective and movie producers were swayed from making any film that would rouse the disapproval of the legion. Thus, for some time, films were effectively censored because of the fear of declining moral values.

Organizations similar to the legion exist today and advocate state, federal and even global regulation of sexually explicit materials. Morality in Media is an organization that campaigns and lobbies against pornography and obscenity. The organization recently promoted a pornography awareness week and distributed white ribbons to wear in support of the "war against pornography." This organization even assists members of certain communities in the fight against pornography. On the Morality in Media website there is information on "how to win against porn in your community" and a publication for sale titled *Win the War in Your Community* which helps citizens lobby for the formal regulation of sexually explicit materials, including Internet content.[14]

Backed by such organizations, many communities have enacted bans on nude dancing and adult bookstores by appealing to a general community interest in morality.[15] Using this same rationale, many are pushing for regulations on Internet content. Support for such regulation was given by the United States Supreme Court in the case of *Paris Adult Theater v. Slaton*[16] where the regulation of adult movies was sought on the grounds of community standards. In the Court's opinion it states, "[T]he States have the power to make a morally neutral judgment that public exhibition of obscene material or commerce in such material has a tendency to injure the community as a whole, to endanger the public safety or to jeopardize ... the States' right ... to maintain a decent society."[17] In *Paris,* Alexander Bickel is also quoted in support of regulation. Bickel believes that obscenity is a problem because it concerns the "quality of life" in a society "now and in the future."[18] In support of this assertion Bickel claims:

> If a man demands a right to obtain the books and pictures he wants in the market, and to foregather in public places — discreet, if you will, but accessible to all — with others who share his tastes, then to grant him this right is to affect the world about the rest of us, and to impinge on other privacies.... What is commonly read and seen and heard and done intrudes upon us all, want it or not.[19]

In short, Bickel and the Court conclude that easy access to sexually explicit materials can harm a community's moral environment. In the next section I will discuss the validity of this claim.

Moral Ecology

The question of whether morality should ever be regulated has been extensively debated and, many authors conclude that, in some circumstances, immorality should be subject to censure.[20] Often the rationale given for this regulation appeals to the public good or "moral ecology" of a society. Robert P. George argues this position. George writes, "someone who has good reasons to believe that a certain act is immoral may support the legal prohibition of that act for the sake of protecting the public morals without necessarily violating a norm of justice or political morality."[21] While some theorists appeal to a perfectionist notion of the "moral good" to defend this position, others rely on the claim that immorality, if left unregulated, will erode the moral fabric of a society and cause unpleasant, immoral conditions to exist.

The basis of the argument that erosion of the moral ecology of a society justifies the regulation of immorality is that, as George writes, "public morality is a public good." Given this claim, George claims, "immoral acts — even between consenting adults — can therefore do public harm."[22] It is because of this harm that George believes societies have reason to worry about their moral ecology[23] and that legislators should encourage moral goodness and "maintain a moral environment" that discourages pornography.[24]

As previously noted, the regulation of pornography and other sexually explicit and obscene materials has often been supported by arguments similar to that offered by George. Proponents of these arguments, like George, argue that ready and easy exposure to pornography, like that offered on the Internet, will alter our attitudes towards sex and each other.[25] This is especially the case, proponents of these arguments claim, concerning children. As George writes, "[P]eople, notably children, are formed not only in households, but in neighborhoods, and wider communities. Parents can prohibit a certain act, but their likelihood of success in enforcing the prohibition, and transmitting to their children a genuine grasp of the wrongness of the prohibited act, will be lessened to the extent that others more or less freely perform the act."[26] While George does recognize that legally suppressing immoral actions cannot make men moral,[27] he claims that a good moral environment can "protect people from strong temptations and inducements to vice" and that a poor moral environment may "seduce people into vice."[28] George writes, "[A] physical environment marred by pollution jeopardizes people's physical health; a social environment abounding in vice threatens their moral well-being and integrity."[29]

As disturbing as the claims made by George (and those who promote similar arguments) may be, this altering of societal morals may not be harmful. In order to be convincing, proponents of arguments like George's must take their claims further and prove that this alteration will be negative and result in harm to society. If such harms cannot be found, the only claim left to make for proponents is that an offensive environment is created.[30] For example, while George claims that immorality will threaten the "ideals of chastity and fidelity," he fails to prove that these ideals are worthy of preservation or should be preserved at the cost of loss of freedom. In fact, in such a pluralist and diverse world, it would be hard to find a basic moral ecology to appeal to as the "right" one or the "good one." If anything, likely candidates for a universal moral good may include a moral environment that supports autonomy, fairness, liberty and/or the promotion of individual freedoms. Therefore, in a morally pluralistic society, it is certainly not evident that any change or alteration in a moral environment (if one even exists) need be worrisome. However, it is still possible to make an argument to the effect that weakening of morality does cause harm. This is especially convincing if it is assumed that morality is the mortar that holds together the foundation of society.

The Hart–Devlin Debate

Patrick Devlin's argument in the well-known Hart–Devlin debate over the Wolfenden Committee report argued that morality does hold societies together. In his argument, Devlin claimed that because of this bond, moral slippage would cause profound social harm. If Devlin's argument is sound, it is possible that the harm incurred to society by the existence of an unregulated Internet may be sufficient to outweigh the harm caused by Internet regulation. However, it will be my conclusion that such an argument cannot be applied to the Internet and fails to justify regulation.

The Wolfenden report, which recommended that homosexuals be allowed to engage their sexual preferences in private, stated that there should be a realm of "private morality" where the law should not intrude.[31] H.L.A. Hart, who looked favorably on the report, argued, along the lines of J.S. Mill's assertion, that if an action does not cause harm, it should not be regulated. Mill writes, "the only purpose for which power can rightfully be exercised over any member of a civilized community against his will is to prevent harm to others."[32] Devlin, who argued the counter position, claimed that private immorality can, in fact, cause harm to society. This is because Devlin believed that a common morality is necessary for the functioning of any society. Of this he wrote:

> For society is something that is not kept together physically; it is held by the invisible bonds of common thought. If the bonds were too far relaxed the members would drift apart. A common morality is part of the bondage. The bondage is part of the price of society; and mankind, which needs society, must pay its price.[33]

Devlin further argued that the loosening of moral bonds is often the first sign of disintegration in society. It was clear to Devlin that, in order to prevent this disintegration, society is justified in taking measures, which some authors may find extreme, to keep its common morality intact. Also, this implies for Devlin that the law is justified in preserving morality "in the same way as it uses it to safeguard anything else that is essential to its existence."[34] This leads to a stronger claim that an act of immorality, because it threatens this essential element in social functioning (the bond of a common morality), is treason.[35] Therefore, even private immorality, by its very existence, threatens the common moral bond and should be prohibited. Devlin's claims are echoed in the more recent words of Tipper Gore. Gore also calls for preservation of a common morality and claims that society rests on a foundation of "shared moral values."[36] Gore argues that we must reassert our values through individual and community action. She writes, "[P]eople of all political persuasions — conservatives, moderates, and liberals alike — need to dedicate themselves once again to preserving the moral foundation of our society."[37] If harm is caused by acts that violate prevailing standards, like the claims made by Devlin and Gore suggest, there may be a strong justification for Internet regulation.

How these prevailing standards were to be ascertained for Devlin is a simple matter for which Devlin used the notion of the man on the Clapham Omnibus. To clarify, Devlin believed that the moral judgment of society should be something that any twelve randomly selected citizens would agree on. Devlin wrote: "[I]mmorality then, for the purpose of the law, is what every right-minded[38] person is presumed to consider immoral."[39] However, Devlin did not believe all immorality should be prohibited. He claimed that actions should be allowed unless they genuinely threatened the integrity of society.[40] Therefore, Devlin did not believe that *just* because an act is immoral it should be prohibited. It had to, according to Devlin, "lie beyond the limits of tolerance."[41] He claimed: "it is not nearly enough to say that a majority dislike a practice; there must be a real feeling of reprobation."[42]

Devlin's argument has been convincing for many, and even Hart agreed that some enforcement of moral principles should be practiced. Also, it seems clear that, at least in the United States, we have laws that serve as moral enforcers. Examples are the laws prohibiting sodomy and suicide. However, Devlin's argument has many flaws and, even if the argument were completely sound and utterly convincing, it could not be used for Internet pornography and obscenity regulation.

Even if it is accepted that some morality is needed to cement the fabric of society, it does not imply that the prevalent morality is what is needed. A moral critic might admit that we could not exist as a society without some morality, while insisting that we can perfectly well exist without *this* morality. Therefore, there is not a necessary connection between the claim that the law may be used to enforce morality and Devlin's (or George's or Gore's) moral conservatism. In addition, Hart rightly argued that Devlin's claim that a weakening of the moral bonds in society is the first sign of collapse is unsupported. Hart wrote: "[N]o reputable historian has maintained this thesis, and there is indeed much evidence against it," and "as a proposition of fact it is entitled to no more respect than the Emperor Justinian's statement that homosexuality was the cause of earthquakes."[43] However, even if all of Devlin's dubious claims are sound, the argument fails when applied to the Internet and modern society.

A Common Morality in the Internet Age?

Devlin clearly saw the roots of the morality he endorsed as that of the Christian religion and believed that the Ten Commandments and the Bible constituted a moral code on which society functioned. He claimed of this infusion of religion into social morality: "[I]t is there not because it is Christian. It has got there because it is Christian, but it remains there because it is built into the house in which we live and could not be removed without bringing it down."[44] Further, Devlin added: "if he wants to live in the house he must accept it as built in the way in which it is."[45] In support of this some commentators see the moral digression in communities as the result of moving away from this Christian structure. Gary Bauer, who was an advisor to the former President of the United States Ronald Reagan and is now president of the Family Research Council, shares these sentiments. Bauer claims that there is an "ongoing cultural civil war revolving around morality" in the United States. Bauer believes that the two sides in this war are those "with fairly traditional religious faith, who see that culture is out of control," and "secular people who believe in a pluralistic society."[46] According to Bauer, those with traditional religious beliefs are clearly in the right, and too much diversity and pluralism are leading the way to the decline of moral values in the Untied States.[47] However, basing morality/legality on Christianity will clearly not suffice in a modern pluralistic world or on the Internet, where users do not share a common background or moral bond. Thus, we are left with the claim that our common morality is disintegrating where no common morality exists.

The problem of trying to enforce a code of morality when there is not a common morality to be found can be illustrated in the following scenario. According to the Christian religion, one of the greatest sins a person can commit is to worship a false idol. For many Christians such a behavior would clearly cause "a feeling of reprobation." However, this does not lead to the conclusion that a ban should be enforced to prevent a Buddhist from meditating while looking at a small representation of the Buddha outside his or her residence. If a common morality is needed, the question remains as to where to find one. This problem is only magnified when considering the Internet. Internet users, even users physically residing in the United States, are from many communities, cultures and religions.

This difficulty has already presented itself in the case of regulating obscenity. The aforementioned case involving the Thomas family is an example. Clearly the "moral code" in California where the Thomases operated their billboard was different from that in Memphis. Also, the "moral code" in small-town Iowa is different than that in New York City. Even the "moral code" that Jones holds will be different than his neighbor Smith. While Devlin could rely on Christianity as a moral backbone, no such backbone exists today and any twelve persons are not likely to agree on what is or is not obscene. Thus, there is no universal moral code to degrade and no basic fabric which pornography or obscenity will erode.

Devlin's method of deciding which acts should be tolerated will also not be successful for the Internet. As stated previously, Devlin believed that what lies beyond the limits of toleration can be judged by twelve randomly selected individuals. However, on the Internet, or in communities of Internet users, this is impossible. If twelve random Internet users were selected, the opinions given would differ widely, especially in regard to pornography and obscenity. For example, in Nevada prostitution is perfectly legal (outside of Las Vegas) and in nudist colonies members routinely walk nude on beaches. However, some Indian and Indian Americans believe that the faces of women should be covered at all times. Therefore, each of these different groups will have a different perception of what is "beyond the limits of toleration." Even in close families there is disagreement. For example, my mother would be perfectly happy declaring most soft-core pornography as "beyond the limits" while I believe that most pornography is well within the limits of toleration.[48] Given these vast differences, it is unlikely that there would be agreement among Internet users or communities in which users reside as to which sites should be regulated due to moral degeneration. An alternative would be to censor whatever sites a user might consider objectionable and likely to harm the moral environment. However, to do this would be to whittle the Internet down to very little content.

Offense and Offensive Environments

Besides moral slippage, there is another way that an unregulated Internet may harm a community. Sexually explicit Internet materials are offensive to many persons and, if widespread, could possibly create an uncomfortable environment. If the offense caused by the widespread availability of sexually explicit materials, such as that offered by the Internet, is severe, it may be grounds for regulation. In this section, I will explore this prospect. Offense, in general, has a subjective connotation and harm an objective one. While someone can claim to be offended, the main evidence for this claim is the claim itself. Being offended is an internal state that is impossible to measure by an observer who cannot quantify the extent of the experience.[49] However, for a claim of harm, the main evidence is not the claim but, rather, some set of observables. However, while offense and harm are not identical, there are cases where extreme offense may create a harmful environment.[50] In such cases, as Nancy Willard claims in her work *The Cyberethics Reader*, the right to a non-offensive environment may supersede the right to view pornography.[51] The Internet, due to the easy availability of sexually explicit materials online, may provide for a similar offensive environment. Therefore, even if an unregulated Internet is not harmful to the moral fabric of society, it could still be argued that much material on the Internet is extremely offensive (perhaps to the point of causing a type of cultural pollution) and that some offensive materials should not be tolerated.

Clearly, offending others is unpleasant and persons with refined manners try to avoid doing so; however, it would be hard indeed to go through life without offending another person. This is mainly due to the variety of things that persons consider offensive. In addition, the enjoyment I receive from doing something offensive may outweigh the unpleasantness caused by someone being offended. Recently, while walking in a rather small town, I took note of many things that could be considered offensive. In just a short walk, I encountered persons with offensive body odor in the form of sweat and large amounts of perfume. I also viewed possibly offensive tee-shirt slogans and persons using what could be considered offensive language. To protect against offense in such an environment would entail the creation of ordinances demanding that persons with body odor bathe, excessive amounts of perfume not be used, offensive tee-shirts be changed and offensive speech be censored. This would clearly be an absurd solution. Instead of impeding the liberties of those who do not wish to wash themselves or those who use perfume and wear tee-shirts with slogans, it causes less disutility for the offended to simply put up with a bit of offense and/or ignore the offending persons or materials. However, there may be cases where offense should be regulated.

In support of the assertion that some offensive speech should be regulated many countries have regulated material, speech and actions that are likely to be offensive. In Canada three form of hate propaganda considered likely to cause offense are regulated — advocacy of genocide, public incitement of hatred and willful promotion of hatred.[52] In the United States some classroom speech at universities is regulated. Recently, at the University of Michigan a student said in a classroom discussion that he believed that homosexuality was a disease that could be treated with therapy. For the offense caused by this statement the student was summoned to a formal disciplinary hearing and accused of violating the school's prohibition on speech that victimizes people based on sexual orientation.[53] The same attitude towards offensive speech can be seen in the case of Carlos Alberto Montaner, a Cuban American television personality. Many Puerto Rican activists campaigned to have Montaner removed from his position after he stated on television that he felt Puerto Rican males contribute to poor economic conditions for Puerto Ricans by leaving the mothers of their children to seek new partners. The representative of the group campaigning for Montaner's removal claimed that Montaner's comments were insulting and that "freedom of speech is not the right to insult a community."[54] Following these examples, Internet regulation could possibly be justified due to offense caused. However, the question remains as to when offense should be regulated.

When to Regulate Offense

One possible answer to the question of when offense should be regulated considers the ease with which the offended can escape or ignore the offense. In general, the harder the offensive material or subject is to escape or ignore, the stronger the case for regulation. In support of the regulation of pornography that is hard to avoid due to offense, Howard Poole writes, "being exposed against one's will to pornography provokes a degree of anxiety which constitutes injury. Therefore, the sort of public display of obscenities to which one cannot reasonably avoid being a spectator constitutes a violation of one's rights and might well justify seeking legal prohibition."[55] This is perhaps true of a captive audience and is supported by the United States Supreme Court. The Court has consistently ruled that the First Amendment does not grant one individual the right to press his or her views on another who is unwilling to listen.[56] Thus if Smith wants to communicate with Jones but Jones seeks to avoid the communication (and no other interests are at stake) the state would be justified in protecting Jones' right to be left alone.

Joel Feinberg includes this captivity clause as one criterion in his "Offense Principle." Feinberg argues that appeal to the Offense Principle may serve to justify state restrictions on individual liberty, but he insists on certain stringent conditions being fulfilled before the offense in question merits restriction. The conditions[57] are as follows:

1. the offense must be a reaction that could reasonably be expected from any person in the nation (or area concerned) selected at random and the offense is not reasonably avoidable,
2. no respect should be shown for abnormal susceptibilities;
3. offenders should be allowed an alternative outlet for their behavior.[58]

While some authors have criticized Feinberg's principle,[59] the criteria are intuitive and (at the very least) provide a good start for assessing when offensive materials should be regulated. However, an immediate objection could be made that Feinberg's third point listed above does not take seriously the interests of all who are offended. Along these lines, it could be argued that even if an offense is "abnormal" it is still a real offense, and the interests of those offended should be counted. This could especially be true when the offense is of a great magnitude.

While this objection may have some merit, I believe that, if taken seriously, the results would be laughable. Persons can be offended by a wide variety of things that, in many cases, say more about the person than the thing causing the offense. For example, I could be deeply offended by any public use of words relating to parts of the body (insofar as all such talk conjures up unwanted and distracting sexual imagery in my mind) and cannot turn on my television without hearing about "piano legs," "chicken thighs," and "turkey breasts." I could also be offended by the sight of tulips or daffodils and file complaints asserting that such flowers should be removed. However, my complaints about these alleged offenses should not be given weight in regard to regulation. The offense that I am exhibiting is most reasonably considered a phobia. As Feinberg writes, "[I]f a mere sneeze causes a glass window to break, we should blame the weakness or brittleness of the glass and not the sneeze."[60] This is not to say, however, that phobic offendees should receive no consideration whatsoever. Rather, the emphasis should be on providing psychological help to them so that they may either eliminate, or learn to live with, their phobic reactions. Thus, the charge that some interests are not taken into account by Feinberg is unfounded. In fact, I believe that too many interests may be given weight under Feinberg's conditions.

While Feinberg does not allow for abnormal susceptibilities to be accounted for, he argues against including considerations of reasonableness with respect to the offense taken. However, it is not clear that some degree of reasonableness should not be taken into account when considering the regulation of offense. It does not follow that just because a reaction could reasonably be expected from any person selected at random, the reaction is reasonable. This clearly has importance for legislation because if it is unreasonable for you to be offended by X, it seems that your arguments for preventing others from performing X will also be unreasonable. Consider a case where a town consisting mostly of homophobic citizens takes great offense at a billboard placed in the center of town depicting a man wearing a pink shirt.[61] Based on the misguided assumption that pink shirts are "gay apparel," the citizens are offended and wish to have the billboard removed. Given that there are no abnormal susceptibilities at work here (if abnormal is a statistical concept), Feinberg's principle seems to support regulatory action being taken against the billboard. However, to support regulation based on such a clearly absurd and provably false concept is dubious. To avoid such regulation the addition of a Reasonableness Condition to Feinberg's criteria may be appropriate. This condition would be similar to Feinberg's condition regarding abnormal susceptibilities and state that offense caused unreasonably should not be counted.

An objection could be made at this point that even "unreasonable" reactions should be given weight and that those who have these reactions are much like allergy suffers. Donald VanDeVeer argues along these lines.[62] VanDeVeer argues that such unreasonable reactions should carry some weight in the application of the Offense Principle by comparing the states of persons offended unreasonably to the distress experienced by persons with allergic reactions. VanDeVeer claims his analogy holds in four respects:

1. Both states involve a characteristic of a person that is a necessary condition for that person's being harmed in a certain way;
2. Both states involve a characteristic presented involuntarily;
3. Few persons have this particular characteristic; and
4. This characteristic may be one that its possessor would be better off without.[63]

VanDeVeer claims that we certainly have an obligation to take the sensibilities of the severe allergy sufferer into account. Given that the allergy sufferer is analogous to the unreasonably offended person in all relevant respects, we also have an obligation to take that person's sensibilities into account. Unfortunately, VanDeVeer conflates two distinct types of offended reactions. While his analogy may hold for some offended reactions which are purely biological[64] it does not hold for many offended reactions.

Many offended reactions are either reasonable or unreasonable, whereas allergic reactions are neither. The negative normative assessment we may coherently make about certain offended reactions cannot sensibly be made in regard to someone suffering from an allergic reaction. As a result, the analogy VanDeVeer wants to run between the two states is problematic. Of course, it could be argued that some offended reactions to, for example, "homosexual" dress are of precisely the same type as allergies. After all, the homophobic person may not be able to give any reasons for his or her reactions. He or she may simply respond to the sight of the attire believed to be liked by homosexuals with a physical disgust not unlike that towards bad odors or spoiled food. To make this analogy, however, ignores a crucial difference. While the disgust of a person offended by "homosexual" clothing is admittedly an unpleasant feeling, it is nevertheless an expression of a view that may be unreasonable. Regardless of whether or not these reasons for the offended reaction can be articulated, they remain expressions that stem from a belief about homosexuality and dress. Thus, some disgusted reactions are indeed expressions of views. They involve reasons, and, accordingly, when offered in support of coercive legislation, these reasons should be subject to public scrutiny.

Feinberg himself states two reservations to the addition of a Reasonableness Condition. His first reservation is that such a condition would be redundant because the "very unreasonableness of the reaction will tend to keep it from being sufficiently widespread to warrant preventive coercion."[65] Clearly Feinberg is too optimistic in this reservation. Reflecting on the history of the United States alone it is clear that widespread unreasonable offense has been taken to things such as the sight of women voting.[66]

Feinberg's second reservation is that the addition of a Reasonableness Condition "would require agencies of the state to make official judgments of the reasonableness and unreasonableness of emotional states and sensibilities, in effect closing these questions to dissent and putting the stamp of state approval on answers to questions which, like issues of ideology and belief, should be left open to unimpeded discussion and practice."67 Feinberg is especially worried that such a condition may take the form of ridiculing what many people believe and that a state determining what things are worthy of respect (what things it is in fact reasonable to respect) would be both dangerous and "contrary to liberal principles."68 While I believe this reservation is weightier than the first, it is still flawed and a reasonableness condition need not be illiberal.

Considering again the case of the town where the townspeople wish to regulate a billboard of a man wearing a pink shirt. There is nothing illiberal with the assertion that the belief held by the citizens of the town is not reasonable. With statistical studies and case analysis it can be shown that not only gay men wear pink shirts. The same would be true if the townspeople were offended by something based on a logical error. The target of the state's evaluation of reasonableness is not a value judgment, it is simply a judgment as to whether the reasons given are coherent and consistent. Given the failure of Feinberg's reservations in cases of this sort, I see no reason why a Reasonableness Condition could not be a useful addition to Feinberg's criteria. While the formulation of such a principle is not within the scoop of this project, what I have shown is that, if anything, Feinberg's conditions may allow for too much regulation. Given this, I believe it is safe to assume that, if something does not meet all of Feinberg's conditions, it should not be subject to regulatory action.

After viewing Feinberg's criteria, it is clear that not all can be satisfied by sexually explicit Internet content. Perhaps the most striking point here concerns the captivity clause. The viewer on the Internet is not a captive audience, and exposure to such material is reasonably avoidable. Given the avoidable nature of sexually explicit Internet materials, it is quite likely that more disutility would be produced by regulation than caused by offense. This is because the offended can easily avoid the offending object. However, the question surfaces as to what constitutes captivity.

In many instances initial exposure to offense will be largely unavoidable. This sort of "captivity" is common. While browsing in a newspaper or switching on the television, an individual may glimpse something that he or she finds offensive. As previously mentioned, offense could also be encountered in multiple forms by simply taking a stroll down a neighborhood street. The same can be said of surfing the Internet. However, it is impossible (and undesirable) for a protective social cocoon to be spun around every citizen. Thus, the true measure of captivity is not in initial exposure but in a citizen's ability to avoid continued exposure to the offense if he or she desires.

Given this distinction, sexually explicit Internet materials are reasonably unavoidable. For most Internet materials, a person can not only reasonably avoid exposure but must actively search for such material. An exception to this is spam[69] that contains sexually explicit images and may be objectionable on these grounds as well as many others. However, most sexually explicit Internet sites are found only by searching and, oftentimes, hidden behind pages that require a user to verify his or her age. Even if a user stumbles upon offensive materials, a click of the mouse is all that is required to make the image vanish.

Another criterion in Feinberg's principle that is not satisfied by most sexually explicit Internet material is the first listed above. As was discussed in Chapter Two, it is difficult, if not impossible, to ascertain which sexually explicit material will be offensive to a randomly selected Internet user or community member. Tastes and preferences vary a great deal, especially regarding sexually oriented material. Given the failure of most sexually explicit materials on the Internet to meet Feinberg's criteria, clearly such material should not be regulated under Feinberg's principle.

To regulate against offense that is easy to avoid or does not satisfy all of Feinberg's conditions would be akin to forcing people to tiptoe around one another and "play nice." In support of the undesirability of such an outcome, Gordon Graham writes, "[C]ould we really have laws requiring us to be kind, generous, or hospitable, and [that] forbade us to be cowardly, vengeful or mean-spirited?"[70] Clearly Graham, like myself, takes the answer to this question to be a resounding no.

7

Regulation: A Bad Idea

Introduction

As I have argued in previous chapters, the common arguments given to support the assertion that harm is produced by unregulated sexually explicit Internet materials fail. Thus, in the absence of convincing arguments, there is little reason to surmise that significant harm will eventuate from not regulating such material.[1] However, on the other side of this equation, I believe there are substantial reasons to believe that significant harm will be produced if sexually explicit Internet material is regulated. The harms that would likely be caused by regulation fall into two broad categories: harms specific to a regulated Internet and harms caused by regulation of sexually explicit material. In this chapter I will examine both categories of potential harms. It will be abundantly clear at the close of the chapter that substantial harm will doubtlessly result from regulating sexually explicit Internet materials. Given the conclusions reached in previous chapters and the harms outlined in this chapter, I will conclude that only vast disutility is to be gained from regulation.

The Price of Liberty

Whenever freedom is suppressed, autonomy is hindered. This is true of the suppression of both actions and speech. By regulating sexually explicit materials, not only is the liberty of those who wish to post such materials impeded but also the liberty of those who wish to view them. If liberty is important and there is value in letting persons make their own decisions, any regulation inhibiting those decisions carries a cost in deprivation of autonomy.[2] This does not, of course, suggest that liberty should always be unimpeded, as there are cases where one's actions can cause immense harm or hinder the liberties of others. In addition, there are certainly situations where the liberty of an individual can be justly impeded if the individual is incapable of making informed decisions.

John Stuart Mill recognized these facts and, in *On Liberty*, he moves from concerns about freedom of speech to concerns over freedom of action. Mill recognized that harming someone may include hindering him or her "in pursuing his own good."[3] According to Mill, not only do persons need freedom of speech to become autonomous (although he never uses this term), they must also be free to conduct "experiments in living." Mill claims that this applies even if others believe that the conduct is "foolish, perverse or wrong." According to Mill, such person-building activities encompass both actions and speech. By living and experiencing what one wants, he or she will be in a better position to decide what is best for him or her. In other words, this is how individuals come to be autonomous decision makers. This requirement of toleration and right to liberty is the basis of Mill's principle of liberty.[4] Of this principle Mill writes, "the principle requires liberty of tastes and pursuits; of framing the plan of our life to suit our own character; of doing as we like, subject to such consequences as may follow: without impediment from our fellow creatures, so long as what we do does not harm them."[5] This principle can humorously be expressed by the old saying "your liberty to swing your arm ends where the other fellow's nose begins." However, this does not imply that self-regarding[6] actions[7] ought to always be tolerated. Mill's principle shows a strong (but not absolute) predisposition towards liberty and justification for the value of liberty. It implies that liberty should be sought whenever possible. In other words, for liberty to be justly restricted, a right must be violated or it must be likely that a violation will occur.[8] As Joel Feinberg writes, "coercion may prevent great evils, and be wholly justified on that account, but it always has its price."[9] This price is the loss of liberty. The price is especially high in a country such as the United States where freedom and liberty are highly valued. Because of this value, considerable injury will result when freedoms are diminished.[10]

Another possible result of restricting liberty, is that a property right may be breached. This is surely the case if individuals own their own bodies. John Locke forcefully justified this right when he wrote, "every Man has a property in his own person. This nobody has any right to but himself."[11] Given that the concept of ownership indicates that those who own something have a claim against all others to leave that thing alone, interfering in what one does with one's body breaches this property right.[12] This is true even if what one wishes to do is view or act in pornographic films or access sexually explicit material. If this property right is important, restricting liberty generates some injury through this violation. Again, this does not imply that it can never be justly breached, only that there is some injury involved in its violation.

Many theorists have taken the ideas of Mill and Locke further to claim that persons have a right[13] to liberty and a right to be left alone. In fact, some authors have claimed that this right is the most basic right or a right that has lexical priority over all other rights.[14] This right has been justified on many grounds. Ronald Dworkin includes liberty as a basic right that must be granted in order to accord everyone equal consideration and respect.[15] John Rawls has justified this right on the basis of fairness, justice and respect for dignity.[16] Loren Lomasky argues for this right because it permits individuals to pursue their own projects and engage in person-building activities in a world of other project pursuers.[17] This list of theorists is nowhere near complete. While each theorist may justify the right to liberty in a different fashion, it is clear that they share a common understanding. This understanding is that violations of liberty (while sometimes just) can result in injury. While some theorists have argued that some rights are absolute,[18] it would be dubious to argue that the right to liberty is absolute even when it causes great harm to others. However, what is probable is that there is damage generated when interfering in liberties. Thus, injury results in the regulation of any material that persons wish to circulate or access.

The Value of Sexually Explicit Materials

Distant from the injuries and possible harm associated with restricting liberties by regulation, it is also possible that some "objectionable" sexually explicit material may contribute value to society that would be lost if regulated. For example, pornography, which is often seen as somewhat of a negative externality[19] of the free market of ideas, may be valuable in many respects. Certainly pornography has value to those who purchase it and, contrary to popular belief, it is not only an inconsequential handful of perverted men who enjoy pornographic materials. Author Sallie Tisdale writes of proposals to regulate pornography based on feminist arguments and the merit she finds in pornography:

> I take this personally, the effort to repress material I enjoy — to tell me how wrong it is for me to enjoy it. Anti-pornography legislation is directed at me: as a user, as a writer.... They look down on me and shake a finger: bad girl. Mustn't touch. That branch of feminism tells me my very thoughts are bad. Pornography tells me the opposite: that none of my thoughts are bad, that anything goes.... The message of pornography is that our sexual selves are real.[20]

Like Tisdale, many women and men find pornographic images to be sexually liberating as well as exciting. As Judith Kegan Gardiner, professor of English and Women's Studies at the University of Illinois claims, "pornography may actually de-objectify women because they can use it to validate their own desires and pleasures."[21] Also, pornography may advance other benefits to its readers. Even the Messe Commission reported that pornography may be valuable to readers by assisting in "the treatment of sexual dysfunctions and the diagnosis and treatment of some paraphilias."[22] Also many couples often enjoy pornography together as a means of obtaining arousal and adding "spice" to their sex lives.[23] Pornography can also be instructional and a person can use pornography for the purpose of acquiring sexual techniques to enhance pleasure.[24]

Pornography may also be valuable as a catalyst for new technologies. In fact, it has been argued that pornography is often the first form of expression to find its way to new technologies. Because of the immense market for pornography, it is a pioneer in providing content using new technology. This creates a market for new technologies and funds future development. In addition, by making new technologies commonplace, innovative applications can be discovered.[25] In fact, the paperback book, cable television and videotape owe much of their success to the consumption of pornography.[26]

In part because of its ability to spread into new markets, between 1500 and 1800 pornography assumed the role of social critique by using the shock value of sex to criticize religious and political institutions and practices.[27] In many ways pornography developed out of the tension between artists and engravers who tried to test the boundaries of the "decent" and those who found such images shocking. This boundary testing is, indeed, a useful tool to facilitate the examination of society. In fact, it is sometimes only when a boundary is raised that we recognize its existence. In many ways much of human behavior is governed by invisible social rules that are only recognized (and thus subject to examination) when they are broken. Consider the common occurrence of meeting an acquaintance on the street. On such an occasion, the acquaintance is likely to say, "hello, how are you?" To this question, the usual reply consists of a brief "not too bad, how are you?" or some other brief statement that usually ends in returning the acquaintance's question. During a short walk, this type of interaction can occur several times and is an accepted incident that is not often spoken of or considered. However, when one of the parties in such an occurrence deviates from the accepted pattern, the pattern becomes clear and is recognized. For example, suppose that Smith meets Jones on the street. Jones says to Smith, "hello, how are you Smith?" However, instead of a standard reply, Smith takes Jones' question into consideration and offers a detailed description of the hemorrhoidectomy that Smith has recently undergone. After the description, Smith proceeds to talk about financial worries and his daughter's impending marriage to a jazz musician. By Smith's deviation from the normal order of things, it will most certainly become clear to Jones that he really had no interest at all in knowing how Smith was doing. In fact, Jones may become somewhat perturbed with Smith. Thus, it becomes apparent what is expected and required of a casual greeting. Sociologist Erving Goffman created a social theory utilizing such "deviant" social encounters. He concluded that sociologists should concentrate on cases where social norms are broken in order to examine what forces uphold the norms.[28]

Performance artist Karen Finley (whose work was denied governmental funding and banned from being performed in many venues because of its sexually explicit content) makes a Goffman-like claim and states that part of the value of her art (and any art) is to be shocking. She claims, "[T]his is my life and I know I'm going to be bringing up controversy, and I think that it would be so much easier if American society just accepted the fact that that's what the artist's job is. To basically bring a mirror to the culture, and turn it around, and make us look at ourselves."[29] Given this view, it is obvious that art can (and perhaps should) make some persons uncomfortable.

Pornography and the shock associated with it deviate from sexual norms and; therefore, like art, can also serve as a heuristic in investigating attitudes concerning sexuality and morality under a Goffman-like theory. Many authors have pointed to this potential value of pornography. For example, Sara Diamond writes, "feminism and porn have something in common. Both insist that women are sexual beings. Both have made sex and experience open to public examination and ... debate."[30] If regulation occurs, the value of sexually explicit materials may be diminished for those who can no longer gain access. In addition to this problem, other materials (with arguably greater value) are likely to also be suppressed if sexually explicit Internet materials are regulated.

The Harmful Application of Regulation

If the Internet is regulated, it is entirely likely that much material that contains artistic and informational value will be lumped in the category "sexually explicit" and made inaccessible on the Internet. Historically, such generalization has been the norm and I can perceive of no reason why it would not be the case in regard to Internet regulation. Some of the greatest works of art could certainly be labeled sexually explicit, inappropriate for minors, morally objectionable and/or degrading to women. If regulation can be justified on the aforementioned grounds, some masterpieces will doubtlessly be regulated. As Catharine MacKinnon writes, "[I]f a women is subjected, why should it matter that the work has other value?"[31]

Examples of artistic masterpieces being subject to censure are numerous and would likely be widespread on a regulated Internet. Recently a reproduction of the Venus de Milo was removed from a shopping mall because the mall managers considered the topless masterpiece too shocking.[32] In another example, Pennsylvania State University officials removed a reproduction of Goya's famous *Maja Desnuda* (The Nude Maja) on the grounds that it made female students uncomfortable.[33] If regulation of sexually explicit materials can be justified on an argument similar to the feminist argument that was appealed to in the previously mentioned case, even the retelling of legends and myths (both pictorially and in writing) would be susceptible to regulation. Such would no doubt be the case of the legend of the Christian Saint Agatha, who was thrust into a brothel and subjected to torture, including the cutting off of her breasts, after she rejected the advances of a Roman governor. Any description or depiction of this legend, such as the painting *The Martyrdom of St. Agatha* by Sebastiano del Piombo, would clearly be a likely target for regulation. Therefore, if sexually explicit Internet materials were regulated many great works would likely become inaccessible on the Internet.

In addition to the injury involved in denying Internet users access to regulated masterpieces, using filters or other methods of regulation may be dangerous. This is due to the fact that some methods of regulation will likely block access to materials such as safer sex information. Safer sex and sexual health information has long been a prime target of censors and would doubtlessly continue to be so over the Internet. Pioneering birth control advocates such as Margaret Sanger and Mary Ware Dennett were, in the past, prosecuted for disseminating birth control information. Such prosecution came about because the advocates were thought to be violating antiobscenity statutes.[34] Also, in the early part of the twentieth century, scientifically accurate information concerning abortion and contraception was suppressed to the point where the only information available was to be found in unreliable underground publications written by "quacks and charlatans."[35] While these examples occurred some time ago, the push to regulate such information continues today. Currently, regulation advocates push for schools to block safer sex information on the basis that it is harmful to children even in the face of teenage pregnancies and the AIDS epidemic.[36] Often the sex-related Internet resources may be the only place that minors can turn for information. This is especially true if they have questions about sexual identity or birth control. In *ACLU v. Reno* the systems operator for the AIDS Educational Global Information System (AEGIS), Sister Mary Elizabeth, testified about the databases that AEGIS is linked with. She testified that for minors "who may not feel comfortable" discussing sex with family and friends, or who "live in areas where they might not feel safe discussing sex with anyone," resources like AEGIS "provide an important venue."[37] Protecting children is the justification often given for regulation; however, for "children" and others who seek such information, not having access to reliable information can have disastrous effects.

Regulation has also traditionally been applied in a biased fashion. Especially vulnerable to regulation have been (and would likely continue to be) information and materials directed at minority populations.[38] While such material may be "shocking" or "gross" to legislators (in the United States legislators are mostly middle-aged Caucasian males), the materials may be helpful and valuable to other populations. Such materials could include safer sex information for homosexual populations. Unfortunately, censorship of materials that contain homosexual themes as well as other materials geared towards minority populations is common. Of this Nadine Strossen, president of the American Civil Liberties Union, writes, "measures to suppress sexual expression consistently have targeted views that challenge the prevailing political, religious, cultural, or social orthodoxy."[39] These views are the opinions and voice of the minority and, thus, minority populations are disproportionately targeted by such regulatory measures. Strossen further claims:

> Because of their subjectivity, current obscenity laws offer a license to the police and prosecutors in any community, or members of any jury,

to punish sexual expression that they find distasteful ... middle-class, middle-aged jurors might well be "turned off" by the erotic rap lyrics that "turn on" poor, inner-city black youth. And heterosexual jurors might well be "grossed out" by Robert Mapplethorpe's gay erotica.[40]

An example of this occurred when Jesse Helms attacked the National Endowment for the Arts for funding work by Robert Mapplethorpe. Helms said, "[T]here is a big difference between '*The Merchant of Venice*' and a photograph of two males of different races on a marble table top ... this Mapplethorpe fellow was an acknowledged homosexual ... the theme goes throughout his work."[41] This sentiment is not unusual. Gay and Lesbian erotica has been extensively attacked and subjected to regulation. *On Our Backs*, a lesbian erotic magazine, has repeatedly been targeted by censors. In Canada, lesbian and gay erotica has, according to Nadine Strossen, "borne the brunt of the censorship."[42] Also in Canada, magazines such as the feminist-lesbian publication *Bad Attitude* have been removed from bookstores.[43] This unequal regulation suppresses minority views and makes any material that is "different" vulnerable to regulation.

Regulation of sexually explicit materials may also divert attention away from substantial harms being produced. As Nadine Strossen writes of regulation based on the feminist argument, "the feminist proposal to censor sexual expression diverts attention and resources from constructive, meaningful steps to address the societal problems at which the censorship is aimed.[44] That is, instead of monies being spent to address educational and economic discrimination and cultural attitudes that lead to the subjection of women, it may be spent on regulation. The effects of such a diversion can include especially detrimental consequences in cases concerning sexual violence against women. Many criminal defendants have pleaded for sentence reductions for rape and other sexual offenses by blaming the availability of pornography for their crimes.[45] If such defenses are accepted and pornography is targeted as the cause of sexual violence, criminals could be pardoned and valuable resources channeled in unprofitable directions.[46]

Internet Specific Harms

Other harms that would likely result from Internet regulation are due primarily to the nature of the Internet. The Internet, like the radio to Meiklejohn, carries with it much promise. It is an arena where one can be heard without possessing a net worth close to that of Bill Gates. Regulation would change the Internet's basic structure and feasibly lessen its potential value. This could transpire in a variety of ways. One likely possibility is that regulation may discourage persons from making ideas available on the Internet that do not correspond with those of the majority. This could fundamentally weaken the potential value of the Internet as a tool for the masses to obtain economic, social and political leverage. This is especially true with regulation utilizing filters that may screen out ideas that are "different." Also due to the nature of the Internet, effective regulation (if it is possible to obtain effective Internet regulation) will only come at the cost of massive amounts of resources and invasions of privacy. In this section I will address these potential Internet specific harms associated with the regulation of sexually explicit Internet materials. When combined with the harms previously discussed, it will be apparent that the potential for harm to result from such regulation is enormous.

As I have previously argued at length, the Internet is unique. In fact, it is not only novel, it radically new. That is, unlike some previous technologies that add a new element to something already existing or increase speed or productivity, the Internet has potentially transformative powers. In his work *The Internet: A Philosophical Inquiry* Gordon Graham outlines the differences between what he believes to be "radically new or merely novel."[47] Graham argues that not only is the Internet radically new, it is akin to a transformative technological revolution. According to Graham, what constitutes a new technology is its ability to provide previously unimagined ways of fulfilling human desires (perhaps even creating some of those desires) and create large-scale alterations in the structure of social and cultural life.[48] The Internet has this potential, especially if unregulated.

The Great Potential

The Internet has the potential to change social and cultural life if information flows remain open. Unlike traditional communications methods, the Internet allows the ordinary citizen to be heard by limitless populations at relatively little cost. It has been argued that this relatively inexpensive speech on the Internet will assist in solving two of the greatest problems facing traditional media: the bias in favor of the speech of the rich and the blandness of much mass media.[49] Also, as many authors assert the ability afforded by the Internet to allow the average citizen to hear and be heard with ease can potentially bring great advantages. Of this potential Gordon Graham writes:

> The World Wide Web is power to the people with a vengeance, we might say since unlike the rather passive medium of television, its interactive character presents ordinary citizens with the possibility of exercising an unprecedented influence on the social and political events that determine their circumstances and prospects. By dramatically extending their control over these public or communal aspects of their lives it gives them a greater degree of personal autonomy than ever before.[50]

Another author, Howard Rheingold, reiterates these claims and writes that the Internet has the "potential to bring enormous leverage to the ordinary citizen at relatively low cost," such as a small listing fee. Given this ease, many E-bay users have become "power sellers"[51] and now sell items at virtual auctions or open online "stores" as a profession.

The possibility of social and political leverage coming about due to the utilization of the Internet is also quite high. This is due, again, to the ease with which persons from all over the world can be heard. If this speech is chilled or made more difficult to access by regulation, this potential leverage will be diminished. When information flows freely on the Internet, persons can be exposed to views and materials that they would be unlikely to access elsewhere. Elizabeth Reid writes of IRC,[52] "[I]t is not uncommon for IRC channels to contain no two people from the same country. With the encouragement of intimacy between users and the tendency for conventional social mores to be ignored on IRC, it becomes possible for people to investigate the differences between their cultures."[53] This expands the social circle for many persons as they become familiar with views and customs quite different from their own. Also, socially, the Internet offers advantages to those with physical handicaps or social anxiety disorders. Persons suffering from such disorders and others may be better able to express themselves in virtual environments where they are accepted in ways they are not in physical communities.

Also, socially and politically, the Internet has the potential to revive a town meeting atmosphere where the ordinary citizen can be heard over professional politicians. Along these lines, Rheingold writes that citizens now have "access to a tool that could bring conviviality and understanding into our lives and might help revitalize the public sphere." This is especially apparent in the way that grassroots blogs[54] are currently transforming politics. A vivid example of the utilization of blogs can be found in the campaign of the 2004 United States presidential candidate Howard Dean. The Dean campaign was actively featured in hundreds of blogs.[55] In a *Wired* article on the use of blogs in the Dean campaign, Lawrence Lessing writes of the potential of blogs. He claims that blogs are "tools that enable, and thus inspire, hundreds of thousands of people to something that American politics has not seen in many years: hundreds of thousands of people are actually doing something."[56] Given the popularity[57] of the untraditional Dean campaign, Lessing may be correct.

Politically, the Internet can also serve as a mouthpiece for traditionally underrepresented groups. For example Rheingold writes, "if a BBS[58] isn't a democratizing technology, there is no such thing."[59] This is because a BBS gives anyone with a computer and modem or other Internet connection the ability to run a business, rant, share ideas, or as Rheingold says, "run it like your own private fiefdom."[60] He also claims that people use such Bulletin Boards to "fight city hall, run for mayor or serve as a sounding board for alternate political views."[61] While BBS technology is not used as much as it was at the time of Rheingold's writing, Internet chat and blogs now possess the same possibilities. Given the tendency of regulation to target minority views, this point of potential leverage is especially vulnerable to being lost to regulation.

Also, the Internet has the ability to remain intact even after traditional communications methods have failed. For example Usenet played a principal role in passing information during the coup in Moscow, and CNN and other Western broadcasters relied on information posted to Usenet. This was because conventional phone and telex channels were "clobbered."[62] Students in Taiwan who had access to Usenet linked to relatives in China to become a network of correspondents during the 1989 Tiananmen Square incident.[63] Also, during the Gulf War the IRC was useful in cross-cultural dialogue. During the war, an Internet link in Kuwait remained active long after television and radio broadcasts ceased, and Kuwaiti students used IRC to offer eyewitness reports.[64] The potential for this type of linkage is only increasing due to the fact that Internet users can now access and download materials from hand-held devices.[65]

Two Objections and Answers

At this point, two obvious objections should be considered. The first objection is that regulating sexually explicit materials need not hinder the free flow of information in other areas or hinder the potential points of leverage. The second objection is that the Internet is unlikely to provide leverage to the masses and/or be influential in changing political and social structures. While both of these objections are plausible, I believe they are mistaken.

While it is theoretically possible that regulation of sexually explicit material need not hinder the democratic and social possibilities provided by the Internet, I believe it will in practice. Clearly regulation could thwart both the democratic and economic promise of the Internet. Also, if sexually explicit material were regulated, persons would be careful in their speech and practice self-censorship. This clearly was the case in Canada in response to the Canadian Supreme Court's decision in *R v. Butler.*[66] In Canada, to be on the safe side, Oxford University Press refused to distribute *Gay Ideas: Outing and Other Controversies* by Canadian philosopher Richard Mohr in order to avoid potential problems with customs. Also, numerous publishers have sent page proofs to

Canadian officials before printing Canadian editions.[67] As reported by the Free Expression Project of the Human Rights Watch, "[T]he indirect effect of daily customs seizures and police raids [in Canada] is self-censorship by the bookstores, video stores and private citizens who for financial reasons cannot afford to mount legal challenges."[68]

Many authors have supported the likelihood that regulation will stifle the potential of the Internet. James Slevin, the author of *The Internet and Society*, writes, "the continual threat of censorship will prevent the Internet from becoming the powerful influence in the economic, social, educational and cultural fields that many hope.... In the long term, such actions can only undermine the trust citizens vest in state authorities. Acts of censorship also continually display the inappropriateness of the 'public good' as a touchstone for the legitimacy of control."[69] Perhaps some of Slevin's concerns can be justified by the fact that regulation has never been, and will never be, precise. In Canada following the *Butler* decision many sexually explicit materials were regulated.[70] Possibly because of the sheer volume of such material, regulation was often done haphazardly and/or by title alone. This poorly executed regulation resulted in two books by one of the strongest supporters of regulation being seized. The books were *Pornography: Men Possessing Women* and *Women Hating* by regulation proponent Andrea Dworkin.[71] Canadian customs officers also seized many works due only to their titles. An example is *Hot, Hotter, Hottest*, which is a cookbook containing recipes for spicy hot cuisine.[72] This sloppy method of regulation is not limited to Canada. Regulating by title alone also occurred in Ohio when *Doing It Debbie's Way*, an exercise videotape by Debbie Reynolds, was blacklisted because the title suggested that it may be a sequel to the pornographic video *Debbie Does Dallas*.[73] Even when regulators look beyond a work's title; many valuable works are sometimes regulated. For example, Canadian customs seized works by acclaimed authors such as Kathy Acker, Langston Hughes, and Oscar Wilde and essays published by a feminist anti-censorship taskforce.[74] Given these recent examples of the effects of regulation, is there any reason to suspect that it will be better when applied to the Internet?

Haphazard censorship can already be seen on the Internet. Currently, the most common method for regulating information on the

Internet in the United States, filters, are notorious for blocking access to materials that are of great social value. Filters are currently required in any United States public library that wishes to utilize government funding.[75] Filters are also commonly used in schools and universities.[76] Websites that have been blocked by filters include those offering information on gay and lesbian rights, an online memorial to Holocaust victims, the HIV/Aids Information Center, Planned Parenthood and many others.[77] This blocking comes about because of several reasons. Some filters simply screen out key words such as, "sex," "fuck," breast," and "beaver." Therefore, when such a filter comes across a site on breast cancer, it disallows access due to the presence of the word "breast." This is frequently quite impeding. Recently, my local news featured a story about a university in Pennsylvania that wished to change the name of its sport team, The Beavers. The desire for a name change was due to the fact that many prospective students could not gain information about the school's sport programs because of filters that block pages containing the word, "beaver." To avoid these problems, some filters only block specific sites; however, these filters also commonly block valuable information. A widespread cause of this blocking is that the sites that filter manufacturers choose to block often depend on the manufacturer's (or group of consultants') subjective choices. For example, Net Nanny, the most popular specific site filter, blocks several pages on gay and lesbian rights.[78]

To argue that the potential of the Internet need not be hindered by regulation is also to ignore the fact that one of the potentially most beneficial aspects of the Internet is its ability to escape governmental control. This lack of governmental control is the reason that many exiled political groups use the Internet to voice concerns and make their political platforms known. To escape governmental control Chinese human rights activists use the Internet to advocate their cause. Also, Tibetan women in exile castigate the Chinese government for its treatment of women still in Tibet using the World Wide Web. This ability to escape regulation gives these groups a voice that allows the world access to their suffering. The inability of countries to suppress citizen speech over the Internet can have great advantages. As Jerry Everard writes, "it is increasingly difficult for countries to get away with systematic human rights abuses. Burma, Peru, Chile, Argentina, China, Vietnam and even Australia have all had human rights abuses publicized as a result of the Internet."[79] An example of this occurred during the conflict in Bosnia when the speech of the Muslim minority in Serbia was greatly repressed by Serbian authorities. Despite the best efforts of the Serbian authorities, the details of the Muslims' plight reached the West over the Internet.[80] If the Internet is made to yield to regulation, cases like this may no longer be commonplace.[81]

The objection that the Internet does not have great potential and, thus, will not be hindered by regulation has been expressed by some authors. Gordon Graham questions the significance of the Internet's power in giving a voice to the oppressed by claiming that knowledge is not always power. An example Graham cites in that of the previously mentioned Muslims in Serbia. Graham points to the fact that although persons in the West were able to access information about the Muslim suffering, they could do little to help. Graham writes of this situation, "[T]hey learnt of the real horrors but their knowledge brought no relevant power."[82] Graham claims the same is true of television and other communications technologies. While I agree that knowledge is not always power, there have been cases where knowledge gained by television and other communications technologies has spurred action. For example, it is plausible that televised images contributed to the success of the civil rights movement in the United States. This could also be argued for in the case of resistance to the war in Vietnam. Imagines are powerful tools. If oppressed groups are not seen or heard, there is simply no possibility of action being taken. An unregulated Internet allows for the possibility that all groups and all persons can be heard. While this potential may not always be realized, the Internet allows for the possibility that it may.

Normative Questions and Technicalities

In addition to stifling the Internet's potential, there is another Internet specific cost that regulation would doubtlessly produce. Many authors are keen to separate the normative question of whether the

Internet *should* be regulated and the technical question of if it *could* be regulated. However, if the only method of effectively regulating the Internet is draconian and/or resource intensive, a normative question arises. To effectively censor the Internet, and "protect" children and others against obscenity and pornography, there would be controls placed on websites, electronic bulletin boards and e-mail.[83] I believe few persons would fail to see the injury produced by their privacy being invaded. All Internet content would likely be scanned and the government would "listen in" to e-mail. While this is not to claim that persons may, at times, believe these measures are justified, they would certainly see the injury produced. Big Brother would have to be everywhere in order to be effective.[84] While there may, possibly (although doubtfully), be a method developed to effectively regulate the Internet and keep adult privacy intact in the future, today's technology does not allow for this workability. In addition, regulation would involve vast resources, effort and time.

Given that it is nearly effortless for one website to close and another to open using a different server, the only way to effectively monitor sites containing pornography and obscenity would involve employing vast amounts of labor and devoting a colossal amount of resources to look for potentially objectionable sites. These resources could be applied in the assistance of the financially impoverished, put forth to help look for a cure for AIDS or used in other humanitarian efforts. Moreover, if regulation, even given the use of extensive resources, would be effective is questionable. While there are no clear lines between what would be an effective method and what would not, I believe that unless very intensive, regulation will make little difference in the amount of pornography and obscenity available. Given that the goal most commonly stated by regulation advocates is to produce a substantial reduction in the amount of materials available to certain persons, unless intensive, regulation will fail.

An objection could be made at this point that, as I have previously argued, even the threat of regulation will cause a reduction in the amount of material on the Internet. From this point it could be derived that the amount of sexually explicit material would be reduced and regulation would be, at least somewhat, effective. While this is true to some extent, it is likely that the threat of criminal prosecution will reduce little of the volume of hardcore pornographic material but a substantial amount of borderline and valuable material. This is because the most law-abiding and concerned will be those who wish to play it safe and avoid prosecution. On the other hand, those who are less concerned with being lawful citizens (perhaps those who traffic in animal sex or child pornography) will find a way around lax regulations. This trend can currently be seen in the "war on drugs" in the United States. While illegal substances are not sold in drugstores and doctors are leery of prescribing (or refuse to prescribe) needed pain medications for fear of prosecution,[85] such substances are readily available in the "shady" parts of town. Thus, while the substances are reduced in many places and their potential to be socially useful diminished, they are still available in such levels that the United States government continues to devote vast resources into fighting this "war."

Those who wish to transfer obscenity and pornography, just as those who sell illegal drugs, will find a way. An example of Internet users finding a method to bypass regulation is presented in Charles Platt's book, *Anarchy Online*. While not philosophical in nature, Platt's example is quite humorous. Platt offers a story of what happened after Senator Exon first proposed to make it a criminal offense for people to say "fuck" and other offensive words online.[86] After Exon's proposal, a software publisher from Idaho made a program for the Macintosh platform called Hexon Exon. The program promised to "Exonize" all texts and make them suitable for Internet transmission. The method by which it did this was to replace all occurrences of the word "fuck" with "Exon." Also words such as "shit," "piss," "ass," and "sucks" were replaced with the last names of other politicians who supported censorship legislation. Thus, the message, "Fuck it! Life sucks!" after running through the program, would become "Exon it! Life Gores!" While the original offensive speech disappears, this would be no more a victory for regulators than transferring the speech into a different language. The offensive meaning remains intact even if the letters are changed. This is just a humorous example, however, the message is clear. In short, those who want to find a way around censorship legislation will. While this is true to a certain extent in all regulation, on the Internet, as the example illustrates, it is ridiculously easy to accomplish.

144

Another example of the ease at which a site can avoid regulation is seen in the current struggle between filter makers and filtered sites. Site makers uncover ways around filters as fast as filters improve. Examples of this occurring include spin-off sites created to avoid filter detection. Changing the name of the URL, a relatively simple process, can create a spin-off site. For example, a site with the URL *www.animalsex.com* could be changed to *www.farmingonline.com*. Once a person enters the new site, they are automatically directed back to the old page. In one small step, this circumvents three distinct types of filters. It bypasses filters that scan subject URLs by changing the subject. It eludes key word filters by changing the key words on the new URL. Also, the currently most effective type of filters, the specific site blocking filters, are ineffective because they rely on a blacklisted directory of sites. Once the URL is changed, the site is no longer on the blacklist.

Another current problem is that most common Internet filters simply do not work to filter sexually explicit material out of peer-to-peer searches. Thus, if I want to circumnavigate current filters, I need only use a peer-to-peer program that has yet to be integrated with filters. New peer-to-peer applications are being released continuously and filter manufactures have not integrated the majority of the programs. While some filters can be configured to block access to all images or all peer-to-peer applications,[87] this solution will squash the great potential of distributed grid computing that relies on such file-sharing. In a congressional hearing addressing sexually explicit materials over peer-to-peer networks, Randy Saaf, president of MediaDefender, claimed, "There is no magic bullets for solving the programs associated with P2P networking. Technologies such as filters will only mildly quash the problem." He also states:

> You cannot look at what every file's content contains, and even if you could, there is a constant state of flux around what files are shared. As soon as you identify one set of a billion files, another set of a billions files will sprout up. That is the nature of networks. Unless a P2P network is centrally run and only allowed to distribute a closed set of content, there will never be a practical technology for preventing "illegal" content while allowing "legal" content.[88]

An objection could be made that, while some distributors may find a method around governmental filtering, many filters will remain useful by blocking some information. Thus, it could be argued that filters are effective tools for regulation to some extent. This, proponents of regulation could argue, is similar to the case of current virus protection software. While it is true that such software is constantly being updated to keep up with new strains of viruses, it is still moderately effective. While this is true, there are two main differences between filters and virus protection software. One difference is that it is very easy to fool filters. This appears to be inherent in the design of all current filters and any foreseeable ones.[89]

Because of this difference, virus protection software developers have some time to work on kinks; however, filter developers have little time before information bypasses their filters. Another difference between virus protection software and filters is in the consequences of changes in the programs. While virus protection software may have kinks and occasionally cause system problems, the effects of changing a filter program are quite different. When a kink is worked out of a filter program, the risk of content that is not sexually explicit being blocked increases. This has historically been the pattern with filters, and the proposed "improved" filters offer little hope for true improvement.

For example, one possible future development in filtering technology involves filtering graphics that contain nudity. Nudity would be measured using a filter that picks out content areas that contain large amounts of graphics with the pigments common in the range of normal skin coloration. This, it is suggested, will be more effective than filters that use key words and lists.[90] However, potential problems are clear. Even if such a filter could be developed, a prospect for which many persons are hopeful, it would filter much content that is not obscene or pornographic. Such content would include fine art photographs and paintings of nudes or those wearing little clothing. Many medieval paintings, such as those depicted in frescoes on cathedral ceilings and walls featuring Jesus wearing only a leaf over his genitals, would certainly be filtered. Pages that have skin colored backgrounds would also most likely be filtered. Also, even graphic filters are fairly simple to bypass by coloring over parts of nudes that are not genitals and/or breasts. Given all the problems with enforcement outlined here and the resources that would be needed, I believe the methods requisite for Internet regulation are so draconian, costly and faulty that the disutility involved in regulation would certainly be vast.

In this chapter I have addressed the probable harms associated with Internet regulation. These harms include both Internet specific harms and those associated with the regulation of sexually explicit materials in general. When this chapter is considered in combination with previous chapters, it should be apparent that there is much to lose and little to be gained by regulating sexually explicit Internet materials. The harms to liberty alone, in the absence of any harm produced by the Internet remaining unregulated, slant the utility equation sufficiently to justify the Internet being unregulated. However, when such harms are united with the potential harms associated with blocking valuable material, stifling the potential of the Internet and the resources and harms involved in the regulatory process, the disutility that will doubtlessly be produced by regulation is clear.

Chapter Notes

Introduction

1. While the Internet is a global medium, most arguments against regulation are country specific (mostly centered in the United States). This is due to the fact that regulation is, at this time, executed only on a country-by-country basis.

2. Burges, Johnson (1948), p. 19.

3. This can be translated as either a *cure* or a *drug*. However, I believe it is most consistent with the tone of the work to translate it as *a drug*.

4. Egypt is generally credited by the Greeks as being the motherland of writing.

5. *Pharmokon.*

6. 274e.

7. 275b.

8. Postman, Neil (1986).

9. Ibid., p. 8.

10. Ibid., pp. 10–20.

11. Writing.

12. *Pharmokon.*

13. Please note that I do not find Plato or Postman's arguments entirely convincing. I merely use them here to show the historical progress of this argument.

14. Mill, John Stuart (1969), p. 21.

15. In Chapter One I discuss many technical aspects that contribute to the unique nature of the Internet.

16. Meiklejohn, Alexander (1948), p. 104.

17. Ibid.

18. See Friedman, Samuel Joshua (2000).

19. This includes both obscenity and pornography.

20. The general assumption made by proponents of this argument is that harms to children deserve special attention. Justifications for such a claim focus on the fact that children are not yet fully autonomous citizens and have not yet developed the ability to act in their own interests. The truth of this assumption is certainly not self-evident.

21. Mainly pornography.

22. Thornburgh, Dick, and Herbert Lin (eds.) (2002).

23. Revenues from adult oriented sites are not reliably known and are hard to estimate. See Rich, Frank (2001).

24. One study concluded that 70 million distinct individuals visited at least 1 adult oriented page per week. See Committee to Study Tools and Strategies for Protecting Kids from Pornography and Their Applicability to Other Inappropriate Internet Content (2002), p. 74.

25. See Devlin, Patrick (1959), p. 12. This debate focused on the Wolfenden Committee report that recommended that homosexuals be allowed to engage in their sexual preferences in private.

Chapter 1

1. "The Declaration of the Independence of Cyberspace," online at <http://www.eff.org.> Barlow co-founded the Electronic Frontier Foundation. The Electronic Frontier Foundation (EFF) is a donor-supported nonprofit organization based in San Francisco and dedicated to defending civil liberties.

2. It is often claimed that child pornography is widespread on the Internet; however, in my research, I have been able to locate very little. This is perhaps due to fear of prosecution and/or the relatively small quantity of such material. I have, however, found sites that have "barely legal" pornography. This type of pornography usually involves youthful young adults of age eighteen or nineteen participating in sexual situations. Often these situations involve portraying the young participants in sexual situations with much older participants.

3. Furniture pornography involves pieces of furniture posed on top of one another with graphic descriptions added. See <http://www.altervistas.com/sites/weird/154>.

4. See Scotland, *Consultation: On the Possession of Extreme Pornographic Material* (2005).

5. ARPA is still in existence and is now called DARPA (Defense Advanced Research Projects Agency). It can be accessed online at <http://www.arpa.mil/>.

6. See the testimony of Mike Godwin representing the Electronic Frontier Foundation, Senate Judiciary Committee Hearing on the Protection of Children from Computer Pornography Act of 1995, 24 July, 1995.

7. Slevin, James (2000).

8. Supercomputers located mainly at large universities.

9. Negropointe, Nicholas (1991), p. 106.

10. These were the three methods discussed in *Reno v. ACLU,* 96–115, June 1997.

11. *Reno v. ACLU* (1997).

12. Popular web browsers include: Internet Explorer, Netscape, Safari and others.

13. See Rheingold, Howard (1993), Chapter 4, "Grassroots Groupminds."

14. Being flamed is the virtual equivalent of being yelled at. This is usually done by the use of all capital letters and harsh words.

15. Rheingold, Howard (1993), Chapter 4, "Grassroots Groupminds."

16. <http://www.runescape.com>.

17. Rheingold, Howard (1993), Chapter 6, "Real-Time Tribes."

18. This type of file-sharing is becoming so popular that in 2002, Northwestern University reported that, at times, 100% of its bandwidth is being used by peer-to-peer programs. See Warning, Sarah (2002).

19. For a more detailed account of the dynamics of peer-to-peer networks see Ripenau, Matel, et al. (2002).

20. Although Napster has been reborn as a more copyright friendly service, the original Napster was forced to shut down its centralized servers in July of 2001.

21. According to Limewire LLC, which develops the popular file-sharing program LimeWire, Gnutella was originally developed by a subsidiary of America Online (AOL). After AOL abandoned development of the Gnutella protocol, programmers downloaded and hacked the software to create their own Gnutella software packages. See <http://www.limewire.com/index.jsp/p2p>.

22. While anonymity is preserved among users, law enforcement agents can identify users' Internet addresses during the file-sharing process.

23. Hayward, S., and R. Batcheider (2001).

24. MediaDefender was founded in

2000 and was, at the time, mainly concerned with illegal trading of copyrighted materials on peer-to-peer networks.

25. See United States (2003), Hearing before the Committee on Government Reform, House of Representatives, 108th Congress, 1st Sess., p. 105.

26. This means that anyone with knowledge of Python (the computing language in which BitTorrent is written) can view the code and explore the programming of BitTorrent.

27. For a detailed summery of BitTorrent see Cohen, Bram (2005).

28. Often when a website becomes suddenly popular, the servers that support it crash. This was famously illustrated when Ken Starr released the Starr Report. When the Starr Report was released the government server that hosted the report was often unattainable because of the large volume of traffic.

29. See <http://www.cacheLogic.com> and Smith, Steve (2005), pp. 79–80.

30. The Linux operating system is commonly distributed by this method.

31. Smith, Steve (2005), p. 79.

32. See <http://www. Atzio.com>

33. Each of these arguments will be explored in forthcoming chapters.

34. Knoll, Amy (1996).

35. 776 F. Supp 135 (S.D.N.Y. 1991).

36. In this case, CompuServe was sued for defamatory messages posted by its visitors at a message forum called Rumorville. The allegedly defamatory remarks included a suggestion that the plaintiff in the case was "bounced" from his previous employer, and a description of the plaintiff's business as a "new start-up scam." The Court held that so long as CompuServe does not know, or does not have reason to know, about the libel, CompuServe cannot be liable. CompuServe was treated more like a bookstore than a publisher, with no editorial control over the content of the message forum. However, it was implied in the case that an ISP like CompuServe could be made liable if it knew of an offending work, but not if it did not.

37. No. 31063-94, 1995.

38. On 28 May 1998, in a closely watched international dispute, a former CompuServe official was convicted in Germany of violating local pornography laws. Felix Somm, who headed CompuServe Deutschland operations until 1997, was blamed for not blocking access to pornographic pictures that were available on the Internet.

39. Martin, Mitchell (1995).

40. The defendant in this case was the owner of a bookstore in California that allegedly sold and distributed obscene books.

41. *Smith v. California*, 361 U.S. 147 (1959).

42. "French Plan to Stifle Internet Freedom." *New Media Age,* 8 February 1996. In this case, Dr. Gubler, who was the personal physician of former French president François Mitterand, wrote a book that described the former president's medical conditions. The book, *The Great Secret,* was published days after Mitterand's death and was banned by Paris judge Jacqueline Cochard after an emergency procedure started by President Mitterand's family on charges of violation of privacy and medical secrecy.

43. This was achieved in the most part by the addition of new amendments to the current Broadcasting Services Act of 1992.

44. See Alston, Richard (2000), for a discussion of the act.

45. NetAlert promotes awareness of Internet laws and encourages citizens to report deviators.

46. What constitutes extreme pornography is somewhat vague. The proposal includes bestiality, sexual intercourse with a corpse, violent pornography and much pornography that is currently con-

sidered obscene in the UK in the definition of extreme pornography.

47. See Scotland, *Consultation: On the Possession of Extreme Pornographic Material* (2005).

48. The government in Singapore is vague about what exactly should be disallowed; however, regulation is not limited to obscenity or hardcore pornography.

49. See Mein, C. T. (1995), p. 35.

50. Ambah, Faiza (1995), and Bogert, Carole (1995).

51. See BBC (2002).

52. This includes sexually explicit material as well as material advocating an anti-government position.

53. See Reuters (2002).

54. Elgin, Ben, and Bruce Einhorn (2006).

55. Ibid.

56. Ibid.

57. CNN and MSNBC recently ran stories on this event. See Wolk, Martin (2006).

58. These include regulations on the times that certain programs can be broadcast on television, proof of age being required to purchase pornographic magazines or enter certain films and other restrictions.

59. See Buckley, William (1998), for a discussion of the outcome of this vote.

60. The Communications Decency Act was designed to protect minors from harmful material on the Internet. Evidence used included Title 47 U. S. C. A.223 (a)(1)(B)(ii) (Supp. 1997), which outlaws the "knowing" transmission of "obscene or indecent" messages to any recipient under 18 years of age. Section 223(d) prohibits the "knowingly" sending or displaying to a person under 18 of any message "that, in context, depicts or describes, in terms patently offensive as measured by contemporary community standards, sexual or excretory activities or organs." A number of plaintiffs filed

suit challenging the constitutionality of 223(a)(1) and 223(d). After making extensive findings of fact, a three-judge district court convened pursuant to the act and entered a preliminary injunction against enforcement of all challenged provisions. The court's judgment enjoins the government from enforcing 223(a)(1)(B)'s prohibitions insofar as they relate to "indecent" communications, but expressly preserves the government's right to investigate and prosecute obscenity or child pornography. The injunction against enforcement of 223(d) is unqualified because that section contains no separate reference to obscenity or child pornography.

61. 47 U.S.C.A. 231 (1999). The Supreme Court decided to uphold a injunction against COPA in *Ashcroft v. ACLU*. See *Ashcroft v. ACLU* (00–1393).

62. The scope of this is very broad and not well defined.

63. Broadcast speech includes television and radio.

64. In this act, Internet communications is placed under the heading "broadcast speech."

65. Regarding the "Protection of Children from Computer Pornography Act of 1995." July 24, 1995.

66. *FCC v. Pacifica,* 438 U.S. 726 (1978).

67. Jaffe, J. Michael (2000).

68. See *FCC v. Pacifica Foundation,* 438 U.S. 726, 748 (1978).

69. See *Red Llion Broadcasting Co. v. FCC,* 395 U.S. 367, 400–401 (1969), and *National Broadcasting Co. v. United States,* 319 U.S. 190, 226–227.

70. What exactly a captive audience amounts to and what qualifies as uniquely pervasive are quite vague.

71. *FCC v Pacifica Foundation,* 438 U.S. (1978).

72. *Denver Area Educational Telecommunications Consortium, Inc. v. FCC,* 518 U.S. 727 (1996).

73. See *Home Box Office v. Wilkinson,* 531 F. Supp. 987, 995–996 n.16 (Utah 1982), and *Community Television of Utah v. Roy City,* 555 F. Supp. 1165, 1172, 1166 (Utah, 1982).

74. The number has to be obtained and dialed and a credit card is often required for users to access this material.

75. A clear exception to this is materials received by spam that may be more akin to receiving obscene phone calls.

76. Information on the Internet can be both easier and harder to access depending on the situation. While initially accessing Internet services may be more difficult than some other mediums, access to specific information, including pornography and obscenity, may be easier once initial access is obtained. Once initial Internet access is obtained, pornography can be accessed without verifying age in some cases.

77. Examples include live chats and video conferencing.

78. The personal computer and the worldwide telecommunication network.

79. Rheingold, Howard (1993).

Chapter 2

1. *Ashcroft v. ACLU* (00–1393). The injunction was upheld in June of 2004. Currently government officials are seeking to challenge the running again.

2. Both Justice O'Connor and Justice Breyer advocated forming a new "national standard."

3. *Stanley v Georgia,* 194 U.S. 557, 558–559 (1969).

4. *Miller v. California,* 413 U.S. 15 (1973).

5. These problems will be addressed later in this chapter.

6. See Schauer, Fredrick (1976), p. 10.

7. Comstock, Anthony (1967), p. 9.

8. Masturbation.

9. Comstock, Anthony (1967), p. 154.

10. Obscenity is never specifically defined; however, it included things such as "dirty" books, pornography, as well as information about abortion and contraception.

11. Comstock, Anthony (1967), p. 13.

12. 3 L.R.-Q.B. 360, 362 (England, 1868). This case involved a pamphlet describing the immorality of Catholic priests.

13. Quoted in Kendrick, Walter (1987), p. 121.

14. Especially of concern here were women, children and those with substandard intelligence.

15. *Regina v. Hicklin,* L.R.3QB 360 (1868).

16. *Roth v. United States, Alberts v. California,* 354 U.S. 476 (1957). In this combined case it was decided that obscene materials do not have constitutional protection. It was also written in the opinion by Justice Brennan that "the unconditional phrasing of the First Amendment was not intended to protect every utterance." In the case, obscenity was defined as that "which deals with sex in a manner appealing to prurient [purely sexual] interest," and that which offends "the common conscience of the community by present-standards." Material having a prurient interest was defined as material having a tendency to excite lustful thoughts.

17. *Memoirs v. Massachusetts,* 383 U.S. 413 (1966). In this case it was decided that obscene materials should not be judged to be without social value just because they are obscene. In order to be regulated, materials must be proven to be *utterly* without social value. There was also a three-prong test developed in this case that closely resembles the current test.

18. This case incorporates the definition of "prurient interest" from *Roth.*

Thus, material that appeals to such an interest is material having a tendency to excite lustful thoughts.

19. What is offensive is not clearly defined in *Miller*. This lack of definition points to much of the vagueness of *Miller* that has paved the way for almost haphazard obscenity regulation.

20. Note that this is a change from the previous definition, in which material had to be proven to be utterly without value.

21. *Miller v. California,* 413 U.S. 15 (1973).

22. Even those that are community based.

23. Alston, Richard (2000), p. 4.

24. See *Paris Adult Theatre v. Slaton,* 413 U.S. 49 (1973), for an example.

25. Linsley, William (1998).

26. *Jacobellis v. Ohio* (1964).

27. Hentoff, Nat (1990), p. 56.

28. And are different among members of a community.

29. White, Harry (1997), p. 2.

30. This is certainly true of colors, which vary depending on the perceiver and the lighting conditions.

31. 418 U.S. 87 (1974). In this case the defendants were tried and convicted of conspiring to mail obscene materials.

32. 413 U.S. 15, 25 (1973).

33. 418 U.S. at 104.

34. Given the lack of a definition of "community."

35. This assumption was due to the precedent set by print media.

36. Robert called new members and took credit card information over the telephone. He also asked for an address and telephone number that he would verify if he suspected that the caller was being untruthful in regard to age.

37. These included photographs of bestiality, nudist camp footage, hardcore pornography (pornography that involves actual sexual acts being performed) and other photos.

38. Like his predecessor, postal inspector Anthony Comstock, Dirmeyer actively sought obscenity in an effort to enforce the Postal Obscenity Law passed in 1873.

39. See Wallace, Jonathan, and Mark Mangan (1997), for a detailed discussion of this case.

40. See *U.S. v. Thomas,* 74 F. 3d (6th cir., 1996), 701, 709–711.

41. Robert served 37 months and Carleen served 30

42. *United States v. Robert and Carleen Thomas,* 94–20019-g, United States District Court for the Western District of Tennessee (1992).

43. Mintz, Howar (1995).

44. Wallace, Jonathan, and Mark Mangan (1997), pp. 10–14.

45. Loundy, David (1994), p. 5.

46. There is much disagreement in the literature surrounding the court's decision. See Petrie, Sean (1997), p. 637.

47. The appropriateness of the court's decision, given the current standard, has been pointed to by many authors. See Lunsford, Brock (1997). Support for the decision can be found in Michael, Jennifer (1997).

48. This problem is not wholly Internet specific as print sources have also struggled with the problem. An example is Larry Flint of *Hustler* who was brought up on obscenity charges.

49. Huelster, Pamela (1995).

50. Martin, Mitchell (1995).

51. Most do not, as sexually explicit material, unlike many goods sold over the Internet, does not need to be mailed to a physical address.

52. Their profits are made mainly by the use of online advertisements.

53. These include the use of public key encryption and remailers.

54. See *The State of Ohio v. the Contemporary Art Center and Dennis Barrie.* The indictment of Dennis Barrie, direc-

tor of the Cincinnati Contemporary Art Center came in the wake of conservative North Carolina senator Jesse Helms' campaign against the National Endowment for the Arts (NEA) for funding controversial art. It was claimed that the Mapplethorpe exhibit, "The Perfect Moment," was obscene. However, the director was acquitted following unanimous support in court from expert witnesses representing the art establishment. Although the jury found that the exhibit appealed to a prurient interest in sex and was offensive, they could not agree it was without artistic merit.

55. Some have claimed that this is exactly what happened in the previously mentioned case involving Robert and Carleen Thomas.

56. Sodom and Gomorrah are ancient cities cited in the Christian Bible as having been destroyed by God due to their wickedness.

57. Loundy, David (1994).

58. Kaplan, Dawn (1998), pp. 189, 194.

59. See Barlow, John Perry (1995), pp. 53–56.

60. Graham, p. 132.

61. See Alexander, Gregory S. (1989), pp. 17–23.

62. See ibid., pp. 24–27, and, Falk, Jim (1998).

63. Rheingold defines virtual communities as, "social aggregations that emerge from the Net when enough people carry on those public discussions long enough, with sufficient human feeling, to form webs of personal relationships in cyberspace." See Rheingold, Howard (1993), Chapter 1.

64. Ibid.

65. Ibid

66. Ibid.

67. Ibid

68. Ibid.

69. Godwin, Mike (1995).

70. This was the case in Lambda-

MOO, and I have personally witnessed this occurrence in other groups. Practically, this involves blocking the user's name on the system. This is, however, often ineffective as the blocked user can just assume another name.

71. See Dibbell, Julian (1996), and Hafner, Katie (1997).

72. A Voodoo doll is a subprogram that can be used in a MOO to attribute actions and responses to characters that the character (or rather the person playing the character) did not originate.

73. See Dibbell, Julian (1996).

74. Rheingold, Howard (1993), Chapter 5.

75. Dibbell, Julian (1996), p. 293.

76. Ibid., p. 294.

77. Gelder, Lindsay Van (1985).

78. This raises many intriguing questions for theories of personal identity, which I, unfortunately, will not cover in this work.

79. In support of this assertion, see Moore, Dinty W. (1995). Also see Mintz, Anne (2002).

80. Rheingold, Howard (1993), Chapter 1.

81. A mythical ring, written about by Plato, that allows the wearer to become invisible.

82. Rheingold, Howard (1993).

83. Ibid.

84. Cherry strudel to be exact.

85. I am, in reality, a tall female with long hair.

86. Loundy, David (1994), p. 5.

87. This is, in large part, due to the inability of any material on the Internet to just remain "local" in any way.

88. In later chapters I will discuss arguments to the effect that such materials may harm the moral fabric of a society.

89. In Chapter Six I will examine the question of whether anything should ever be subject to regulation on the grounds of its perceived immorality.

Chapter 3

1. See United States Constitution, Amendment I. This has been interpreted many ways. I will discuss some of these interpretations later in this chapter.

2. There is much debate as to the coverage and strength of the protection that should be given to speech. To a large extent what a theorist believes should be within the coverage of the First Amendment depends on the justifications he or she uses for upholding it. An example I will discuss is Alexander Meiklejohn, who argued for absolute coverage and protection for political speech. Meiklejohn justified such protection on the grounds of the functioning of democracy, thus, his absolute coverage was limited to political communication.

3. It should be noted that I will not be arguing for censorship. I will merely argue that the current justifications for upholding free speech are not sufficient for the protection of sexually explicit Internet materials.

4. Parts of Jefferson's diary have been published in several forms; see Jefferson, Thomas (1999).

5. See Franklin's autobiography at <http://www.ushistory.org/franklin/autobiography/index.htm>.

6. Meiklejohn, Alexander (1948), p. 4.

7. Ibid., p. 10. Note that he claims it is an absolute only in regard to public speech.

8. Ibid., p. 17.

9. Cohen, Myer (1937), p. 4.

10. There are many historical cases to support these findings. See *Beauharnais v. Illinois*, 343 US 250, 252 (1952) (libel); *Collins v. Smith,* 447 F. Supp. 676 (ND III. 1978) (fraud); *Rice v. Paladin Enterprises* Inc., No. 96–2412, 128 F. 3d 233 (10 November 1997) (incitement to commit murder); and *Parminter v. Coupland* (1840), GM&W 105 at 108 (libel and slander); for a few examples.

11. This is the definition used in many philosophical works on free speech and in many legal cases. Examples include Fredrick Schauer (1982) and Wojciech Sadurski's *Freedom of Speech and Its Limits*. A few examples of the definition being employed in legal cases in the United States are *Jarman v, Williams*, 753 F. 2d 76, 78 (8th Cir. 1985), and *Sunset Amusement Co. v. Board of Police Comrs. of City of Los Angeles*, 7 Cal. 3d 64, 74 496, p. 2d 840, 845–846.

12. Schauer, Fredrick (1982), p. 98.

13. See Kurland, Philip B. (1975), for an interesting history of Supreme Court decisions regarding free speech.

14. Note that if taken to an extreme, this assumption of fallibility could justify noninterference in even harm-causing conduct. This is because if we are truly this fallible, we may be wrong to allege that some conduct causes harm and are not in a position to interfere.

15. A belief that may contain either elements of the truth but not the entire truth or untrue elements.

16. New York: Simon and Schuster, 1996.

17. Note that I am dubious that a government could successfully squash such claims, especially with the ability of Internet speech to escape governmental regulation that I will discuss in the closing chapter. However, the point remains that there may be interests that are more important than truth when considering speech regulation.

18. A view I do not advocate.

19. I am not claiming here that all academic disciplines live up to such an ideal, only that, ideally, they presuppose such a view.

20. I am assuming in this case that there is not an actual fire in the building and that the person speaking does not believe there to be.

21. Please note that this can be applied to most but not all of the sexually

explicit Internet materials targeted by regulators. There have been many artistic works labeled as "obscene" in the past where truth may be a concern. However, I believe the arguments given earlier in this chapter give reason to be suspicious of the argument from truth applied to any work targeted for regulation.

22. In Chapter Five I will present arguments made by feminists that pornography and obscenity "say" something about women. If this is true, truth is, perhaps, a relevant argument. However, I will argue that this is not the case.

23. See Scanlon, Thomas (1972), pp. 204–226.

24. Rawls, John (1971).

25. Obviously this does not imply that they must be equal in all respects. This is confined to their voice as citizens and not to all material possessions or abilities.

26. He also argues, more controversially, that the parties would prefer a distribution of basic goods that would tolerate inequalities (because inequalities provide incentives to production) only when those inequalities raise the level of the least well off. This is Rawls' famous "difference principle."

27. This is because if persons were behind the veil of ignorance they would want speech to be free.

28. While it may be possible to carve out a category of intimate actions and speech that should be protected, I believe this will not be a sufficient solution. If we were to include intimate actions in some type of free speech category, consensual sexual relations performed in a public place and other similarly offensive actions would be protected. This may be an undesirable consequence.

29. Scanlon, Thomas (1972), pp. 204–226.

30. Ibid., p. 217.

31. Scanlon, Thomas M. (1979), p. 532.

32. While autonomy is taken to be valuable, perhaps even super-valuable, and serves to structure and guide many contemporary debates, it has come to mean many different things to many different philosophers. In *Harm to Self,* Joel Feinberg identifies several senses of autonomy and Gerald Dworkin has claimed that autonomy is merely a philosopher's "term of art"; Dworkin (1988). However, Dworkin aside, it may be possible to identify a core concept of autonomy upon which these varying conceptions are based. Fortunately, the question of what autonomy is has received a great deal of philosophical attention in recent years. This largely stems from the publication in 1971 of Harry Frankfurt's paper "Freedom of the Will and the Concept of the Person"; Frankfurt (1971). For Frankfort, in order for my first-order desires to be autonomous they must be endorsed by my second-order desires. Although the above model of autonomy has been enormously influential, it has also been subject to penetrating criticisms, in the light of which both Frankfurt and others have modified it. In his Presidential Address to the American Philosophical Association, Frankfurt reformulated his definition of autonomy through appeal to the notion of "satisfaction." On this account, a person identifies with a desire if it is endorsed by a higher-order desire with which the person is satisfied. Satisfaction here merely means that one has no interest in trying to change his or her motivation.

33. This is of course debatable; however, most theorists assume it to be the case.

34. Another version of this argument focuses on one aspect of person building: a general attitude towards tolerance. See Bollinger, Lee (1980).

35. Scanlon, Thomas (1972), pp. 215–216. It should be noted, however, that Scanlon later expressed doubts on the validity of this earlier argument.

36. Chapter 20, *Ostenditure in Libra Republica Unicuique et Sentire Quae Velit, at Quae Sentiat Dicere Licere* (In a free state everyone may think what he pleases and say what he thinks). The claim is that freedom of thought is aided by freedom of speech.

37. It should be noted again that I am not advocating censorship here. I am merely pointing out the flaws in the common arguments for free speech.

38. It may well be possible to argue for a special status for speech and intimate actions.

39. Perhaps the most famous is that offered by Meiklejohn; however, modern versions and applications of this argument have also arisen. For example see Ely, J. (1980), pp. 105–136.

40. Meiklejohn, Alexander (1948), p. 66.

41. Ibid., p. 88.

42. Ibid. p. 42. Private speech, for Meiklejohn, is speech that does not discuss the public interest.

43. Ibid., p. 39.

44. Note that I am talking only of graphic pornography here. There are clearly cases where a work of art may induce sexual stimulation as well as other emotions, feelings and thoughts.

45. Examples of this are numerous and include the condemnation of Galileo for asserting that the solar system was heliocentric as well as the banning of many books such as *Ulysses*.

46. Cox, Phil (1997).

47. Quoted in Schauer, Fredrick (1982), p. 83.

48. Feinberg, Joel (1992), p. 192.

49. Bork, Robert (1997).

50. In this case it is possible that the communication involves several communicators depending on who has the intent to communicate.

51. This phrase is common in many Supreme Court decisions relating to freedom of speech.

52. See Mill. John Stuart (1969), in Chapter Three. Here Mill claims that the opinion that corn-dealers are starvers of the poor should be unrestricted in the press; however, if this opinion is delivered in front of an angry mob, it should be restricted.

53. Schauer, Fredrick (1982), p. 205.

54. Smolla, Rodney A. (1992), p. 14.

55. Ibid.

56. The position that free speech is necessary for a democracy to function.

57. Smolla here is claiming that those who hold this position are acting in an elitist fashion towards speech that is not political and, by implication, those who wish to communicate such speech. Ibid. pp., 15–16.

Chapter 4

1. Exon, Jim (1998), p. 46.

2. Hearing before the Subcommittee on Telecommunication, Trade and Consumer Protection of the Committee on Commerce, House of Representatives, 105th Congress, 2nd Sess., on H.R. 3783, H.R. 774, H.R. 1180, H.R. 1964, H.R. 3177, and H.R. 3442; Serial No. 105–119.

3. There were 17 plaintiffs listed in this challenge including the American Civil Liberties Union.

4. Addicted to Noise (1999).

5. Personal Responsibility and Work Opportunity Reconciliation Act of 1996, PL 104–93, 104th Congress, 42, U.S.C. 710 (1996).

6. The defendant owned a lunch counter and sold two "girlie" magazines to a 16-year-old boy.

7. *Ginsberg .v New York,* 290 U.S. 629 (1968.)

8. There is not a specific legal definition of harm.

9. *Miller v. California* 413 U.S. (1973).

10. This can be defined as sexual or leading to sexual arousal.

11. This implies that it must be clear that it is offensive.

12. Davidson, Sandra, and Betty Houchin Winfield (1999), p. 14.

13. Ibid.

14. Everard, Jerry (2000), p. 142.

15. Feinberg, Joel (1984), p. 105. An interest is something that someone wishes to advance. This is not to be confused with desires, as it is often possible to have an interest in something, one's health for example, and not actively desire it.

16. As I will argue later in the chapter, I do not believe that harm need occur at all. However, possible harms may include confusion or, in the aftermath, coping with the parental response that may occur.

17. I will outline the harm produced by regulation in Chapter Seven.

18. Hearing before the Subcommittee on Telecommunication, Trade and Consumer Protection of the Committee on Commerce, House of Representatives. 105th Congress, 2nd Sess., on H.R. 3783, H.R. 774, H.R. 1180, H.R. 1964, H.R. 3177, and H.R. 3442; Serial No. 105–119.

19. For an example, see McPhee, Mike (1998).

20. See the statement of Stephen R. Wiley of the Federal Bureau of Investigation, in Hearing before the Subcommittee on Telecommunication, Trade and Consumer Protection of the Committee on Commerce, House of Representatives, 105th Congress, 2nd Sess., on H.R. 3783, H.R. 774, H.R. 1180, H.R. 1964, H.R. 3177, and H.R. 3442. Serial No. 25–30.

21. See <http://www.safekids.com>.

22. It should be noted that I am not so overly optimistic as to suggest that parental supervision will be perfect and prevent all further instances of such activities. However, I do believe that rely-ing on such supervision will produce less disutility than denying access to such areas. This is the case in many public spaces. Parents are relied upon to supervise their children in malls or parks. While this supervision is not always perfect, it works most of the time and produces less disutility than not allowing access to such places.

23. Veyne, Paul (1987), p. 79.

24. See Pagels, Elaine (1988).

25. McLaughlin, Mary Martin (1974), p. 111.

26. Aries, Philippe (1962), p. 103.

27. See Tissot, Samueal-Auguste (1766), p. 22.

28. Gay, Peter (1984), p. 304.

29. Bertin, Joan (1998), p. 3, quoting Judy Blume.

30. Poole, Howard (1982), pp. 39–44.

31. Pornography has many definitions but most center on the sexually explicit nature of such material. Obscenity, on the other hand, is a legal term that has been defined in *Miller v. California*. This definition can be found in the previous chapter.

32. Layden is rather vague on some aspects of this case.

33. It is implied that this addiction occurred because of exposure to common magazines such as *Playboy*.

34. See Legislative Proposals to Protect Children From Inappropriate Materials on the Internet, p. 53.

35. Ibid., p. 85.

36. Ibid.

37. Common examples are Net Nanny, Safe Surf and Cyber Sitter.

38. E-mail sent to bulk addresses usually intended to sell or advertise a product or service. These sometimes contain rather lewd pornographic images or deal with "adult" subjects such as penis enlargement.

39. Poole, Howard (1982), p. 43.

40. One possible exception to this is where child pornography is used to teach

children that sexual acts between adults and children are normal. However, child pornography in any form is objectionable for reasons apart from the effects it may have on a viewer and should be illegal for these reasons alone. See Tyler, R. P., and L. E. Stone (1985), pp. 313–318.

41. White, Harry (1997), p. 48.

42. Everard, Jerry (2000).

43. Anderson, Ray (1999), p. 219.

44. I will discuss the relationship between harm to women and pornography in the following chapter.

45. Presidential Commission on Obscenity and Pornography, 1970. Quoted in White, Harry (1997), p. 46.

46. See Burger, Robert H. (1987); Smith, Tom W. (1987); and Wilcox, Brian L. (1987); for support.

47. Attorney General's Commission on Pornography (July 1986).,

48. Ford, M. E., and J. A. Linney (1995), pp. 56–76.

49. Howitt, D. (1995), pp. 5–27.

50. This last variable is particularly important given that the reward of masturbation could, using classical conditioning theories, be a strong incentive for pornography to become associated with pleasure and thus be reinforced in children.

51. Howitt, D. (1995), p. 20.

52. Quoted in Heins, Majorie (1999).

53. Effects last about two hours.

54. See Myers, David (1992), for a breakdown of these studies.

55. See Patterson, G. R., et al. (1991).

56. See Malamuth, N. M., and J. P. Check (1981), pp. 436–446.

57. See Eron, L. D., and L. R. Huesmann (1980), pp. 319–331, and, Parke, R. D., et al. (1964).

58. Lloyd, Margaret A., and Wayne Weiten (1994).

59. Intons-Peterson, M. J., et al. (1989), pp. 256–275.

60. This software allows parents to read e-mail and record chat messages and passwords.

61. Aftab, Parry (2000), p. 57.

62. The actual claim is that exposure to pornography leads to sex offenses in general.

63. Langevin, R., and R. A. Lang (1985), pp. 403–419.

64. Kuthchinsky, B. (1973).

65. Knudsen, D. D. (1988).

66. This case concerned signal bleed from premium adult cable channels.

67. Brief for Appellants in *U.S. v. Playboy Entertainment Group*, S.Ct. No. 98–1682 (August 1999), pp. 38–40.

68. White, Harry (1997), p. 6.

69. Ibid., pp. 83–84.

70. Michener, Andrew, and John D. Delamater (1994).

71. Plagen, Peter (1991), p. 46.

72. Of course this concern for enforcement would be argued for on the basis that people are harmed by their morals being degraded. This line of argumentation will be examined in Chapter Six.

Chapter 5

1. Longino, Helen E. (1998), p. 125.

2. Many claim that this subordination is degrading to women; however, MacKinnon seems to use *subordination* in many different ways. In general, when something subordinates women it tends to perpetuate the subordinate status of women in society that leads to differences in pay, insults and injury at home and negative attitudes concerning women.

3. Dworkin, Andrea, and Catharine MacKinnon (1988), pp. 138–142.

4. My thanks to Theodore Gracyk for providing this excellent example.

5. MacKinnon, Catharine A. (1985).

6. Erotica often includes an element of artistic merit in its definition. For example, see Steinem, Gloria. (1998).

7. Dworkin, Andrea (1993), p. 94.

8. Judy Chicago's work would be a possible example.

9. While the main concern here seems to be dehumanization of women due to fragmentation, there is not a reliable way of knowing when a focus on body parts "reduces" women to those body parts. Also, the ordinance constructed by Mac-Kinnon provides no guidance in dealing with this problem.

10. This even includes non-violent as well as lesbian and gay pornography.

11. An example is where she writes, "the women used in pornography are used in pornography" while defining pornography as that which, essentially, uses women, in *Pornography: Men Possessing Women*, p. 201.

12. She does not offer a precise definition of harm. However, when she speaks of harm, she focuses on the degrading nature of pornography.

13. It is interesting to note here that she includes lesbian pornography made by female pornographers involving only females.

14. Dworkin, Andrea (1979), p. 200.

15. Note here that this remark incorporates many of Dworkin's ideas that viewing pornography is akin to men "fucking women in their head"; see Dworkin, Andrea (1993).

16. MacKinnon, Catharine (1993), p. 9.

17. This could be done in a number of ways, however, the most common claim is that they are treated in a degrading fashion and used merely as means.

18. The actress that stared in the movie *Deep Throat*. Note that Linda Lovelace has now retracted her story and claims that she was never abused in the pornography industry. See Strossen, Nadine (1995), pp. 182–184.

19. MacKinnon, Catharine (1993), p. 21.

20. A person's desire is autonomous if he or she decides to treat that desire as providing a reason to act, and if he or she is satisfied with this decision. More-over, this desire must not have been inculcated into the agent through any illegitimate external interference with her motivational set.

21. Quoted in Tanenbaum, Leora (1994.)

22. See <http://www.ffeusa.org/html/speakers/royalle.html > and <http://www.ffeusa.org/html/speakers/leonard.html>.

23. Pornography that depicts acts of violence, usually against women. This is to be distinguished from "snuff" films, where actual violence is inflicted on women or men.

24. See Hill, Judith (1998).

25. This is a female run pornography production and distribution company. The films from Femme Productions are often characterized by their creator, Candida Royalle, as movies to teach men how to make love to women.

26. Blush productions specializes in lesbian erotica.

27. Currently there is not a universal consensus on the working conditions present in the pornography industry.

28. Royalle, Candida (1993), pp. 23–32.

29. I thank Rural Opportunities in Bowling Green, Ohio, for providing information concerning the working conditions of migrant crop workers.

30. In Denmark, sex workers are unionized.

31. Quoted by Walter Gellhorn. See Gellhorn, Walter (1956), pp. 60–61.

32. Strossen, Nadine (1998), p. 58.

33. For a comprehensive review of the social science data, see Pally, Marcia (1994).

34. Dority, Barbara (1989), p. 151.

35. Langevin, R., et al. (1988).

36. Fischer, W. A. (1994), pp. 23–38.

37. Padgett, V. R., et al. (1989).

38. Reported in *Glamour*, April 2002, p. 8.

39. Dority, Barbara (1989), p. 153.

40. Feinberg, Joel (1985), p. 152.

41. Kutchinsky, B. (1991), pp. 47–64.

42. Diamond, Milton, and Uchiyama, Ayako (1999).

43. Buruma, Ian (1984), p. 55.

44. Baron, L. (1990).

45. Padgett, V. R., et al. (1989), pp. 479–491.

46. Carter, D. I., et al. (1987).

47. Kutchinsky, B. (1973), pp. 163–181.

48. Rauch, Jonathan (1998), p. 32.

49. Perhaps because of cultural attitudes towards women.

50. MacKinnon, Catharine (1993), p. 21.

51. Brod, Harry (1988), pp. 114–121.

52. MacKinnon, Catharine (1993), p. 26.

53. Ibid., p. 17.

54. Ibid.

55. Orwell, George (1949), p. 161.

56. MacKinnon, Catharine (1993), p. 13.

57. Ibid., p. 14.

58. Ibid., p. 15.

59. Ibid., p. 58.

60. Hill, Judith (1998), p. 108.

61. Ibid., p. 110.

62. An example can be found in the popular television serious *Roots*.

63. The purposeful departure from reality is what differentiates pornography and other forms of pure fantasy from many television programs and films that are reality-based.

64. A fantasy is a product of the creative imagination that departs from the space of reality in a creative way and can be conceived in the mind or expressed (as in a work of art).

65. Please note that I am not claiming the existence of any causal correlation between such material and harm.

66. Christensen, F. M. (1990), p. 259.

67. In this case, the petitioner was convicted in a state court for distributing on the streets of Chicago anti–Negro leaflets in violation of Ill. Rev. Stat., 1949,

c. 38, § 471, which makes it a crime to exhibit in any public place any publication which "portrays depravity, criminality, unchastely, or lack of virtue of a class of citizens, of any race, color, creed or religion" which "exposes the citizens of any race, color, creed or religion to contempt, derision, or obloquy."

68. *Beauharnais v. Illinois*, 343 US 250, 252 (1952).

69. *New York Times v. Sullivan*, 376 US 254, 279–280 (1964). In this case, the respondent, Sullivan, an elected commissioner of the city of Montgomery, Alabama, alleged that he had been libeled by statements in a full-page advertisement that was carried in the *New York Times* on March 29, 1960, entitled "Heed Their Rising Voices." This was a fundraising advertisement for the civil rights movement. The ad contained several minor errors of fact. Sullivan sued the *New York Times* for libel, claiming that the ad referred to him in that he oversaw the Montgomery Police Department that was mentioned in it. Ruling against Sullivan, the Supreme Court concluded that allowing libel lawsuits in cases like this one would "chill" future criticism of government officials and that a "pall of fear and timidity" would fall over speakers, leading to "'self-censorship." Because of these concerns, the Supreme Court ruled that a "public official" may not recover "damages for a defamatory falsehood relating to his official conduct unless he proves that the statement was made with 'actual malice' — that is, with knowledge that it was false or with reckless disregard" of the truth.

70. See *Nationalist Socialist Party v. Skokie*, 432 US 43 (1977). In this case, permission was granted to the Nationalist Socialist Party (a Nazi-like organization which preaches anti–Semitism) to march in a predominately Jewish neighborhood.

71. Longino, Helen E. (1998), p. 125.

72. Dworkin, Ronald (1977), p. 208.

73. Langton, Rae (1993), pp. 292–330.

74. MacKinnon, Catharine (1993), p. 9.

75. Dority, Barbara (1989), pp. 152–153.

76. Feinberg, Joel (1985), p. 151.

77. Ibid., p. 158.

78. Pateman, Carole (1988).

79. In fact, as the previously mentioned studies tend to conclude, there is some evidence that the availability of pornography is actually linked with positive attitudes towards women.

80. Quoted in Strossen, Nadine (1995), p. 174.

Chapter 6

1. Also referred to as moral ecology.

2. Bork, Robert (1997).

3. While Bork does not concentrate solely on Internet pornography and obscenity, he does see the Internet as the latest step towards "Gomorrah."

4. Bork, Robert (1997), p. 383.

5. Layhaye, Tim (1998).

6. Will, George F. (1990).

7. Elias, James (1999).

8. Associated Press of Washington, *Toledo Blade*, 30 January 2002, A3.

9. The concern was that they would become consumers of pornography and be "corrupted" and "mentally poisoned."

10. Quoted in Hafferkamp, Jack (1999).

11. Note that this was before the terrorist attacks in the United States of September 11, 2001.

12. See the statement by Michael Oxley in the Hearing before the Subcommittee on Telecommunication, Trade and Consumer Protection of the Committee on Commerce, House of Representatives, 105th Congress, 2nd Sess., on H.R. 3783, H.R. 774, H.R. 1180, H.R. 1964, H.R. 3177, and H.R. 3442; Serial No. 105–119.

13. Friedman, Joshua (2000).

14. See http://www.moralityinmedia.org.

15. See *Barnes v. Glen Theatre, Inc.* (90–26), 501 U.S. 560 (1991). In this case it was decided that not all nude dancing is entitled to First Amendment protection and that communities can regulate dancing on the grounds of a community interest in morality.

16. *Paris Adult Theatre v. Slaton* 413 U.S. 49 (1973). The Court's opinion in this case suggests that there is a "right of the Nation and of the states to maintain a decent society." Do note that nowhere in this case is empirical evidence presented or discussed to support the assertion that such material may actually cause any of the aforementioned problems.

17. *Paris Adult Theatre v. Slaton,* 413 U.S. 49 (1973).

18. Bickel, Alexander (1971), p. 25.

19. *Paris Adult Theatre I,* 413 U.S. at 59, quoting Alexander Bickel.

20. On the other end of this debate, some theorists argue that moralistic laws are unjust and that morality should never be the subject of regulation.

21. George, Robert P. (1993), p. viii.

22. Ibid., p. 36.

23. Ibid., p. 37. I take George here to mean the moral environment in which we live and make moral decisions although he does not precisely define this concept.

24. Ibid., p. 43.

25. Fred Berger gives a proficient summery of some of the claims of proponents of this argument in Berger, Fred (1977).

26. George, Robert P. (1993), p. 27.

27. This is assuming that morality involves both external and internal states.

28. George, Robert P. (1993), p. 45.

29. Ibid.

30. I will address offense later in this chapter.

31. Hart, H. L. A (1963), p. 14.

32. Mill, John Stuart (1859), in Chapter 1. Do note, however, that harm alone may not constitute a reason for regulation.

33. Devlin, Patrick (1959), p. 20.

34. Ibid., p.10

35. This is because it is an affront against the fabric of society.

36. Gore, Tipper (1987).

37. Ibid., p. 12.

38. While "right-minded" may seem to violate the principles of random selection, Devlin is using right-minded to represent persons who do not suffer from medical conditions that may impair judgment. Thus, persons who are developmentally delayed and/or suffer from some mental disorders would be excluded from the selection process.

39. Devlin, Patrick (1959), p. 15.

40. In other words, undermine the common moral base.

41. Devlin, Patrick (1959), p. 118.

42. Ibid., p. 7.

43. Hart, H. L. A. (1963), p. 50.

44. Devlin, Patrick (1959), p. 9.

45. Ibid.

46. Quoted in Strossen, Nadine (1998), p. 49.

47. Ibid.

48. Do note, as previously mentioned, that I consider child pornography to be objectionable for reasons apart from its content.

49. Even psychological harms can usually be measured quantitatively by changes in the body. These changes include those in heart rate, common bodily signs of stress as well as changes in appetite and sleep patterns.

50. I hasten to point out, however, that there remains a great deal of unresolved confusion in the literature over the extension of both "offensiveness" and "harmfulness." This has been a nettlesome problem for some time, a problem that can perhaps be traced back to Mill's

famous "exception" allowing for legislation to prohibit "offenses against indecency"; On Liberty, p. 99.

51. Willard, Nancy (1997).

52. Cotler, Irwin (2000).

53. Rauch, Jonathan (1998), p. 7.

54. Ibid., p. 38.

55. Poole, Howard (1982), p. 42.

56. See Schneider v. State, 308 U.S. 147 (1939); Martin v. City of Struthers, 319 U.S. 148 (1943); Rowen v. Post Office, 397 U.S. 728, 736–737 (1970).

57. Note that in Offense to Others Feinberg has revised some of these points and incorporated his principle into a balancing metaphor. In this he claims that we must weigh both sides in a particular case of alleged offense to determine what the state's role ought to be. Both the offended parties' and the offending parties' interests should be taken into account. In weighing interests, we should consider the following three factors: (1) the importance of the "offending" conduct, both to the "offender" and to society at large; (2) the possibility that the "offending" conduct might have been performed at times/places causing less or no offense; and (3) the extent, if any, to which the offense is caused with spiteful motives. Thus, if my offensive conduct is of great social utility, could not have been performed at any other place/time, and was done with no spiteful motives, the considerations involved on the side of those offended must be extremely weighty to override my interests and justify intervention. See Feinberg, Joel (1985), p. 26.

58. Feinberg, Joel (1980), p. 70.

59. See Manning, Rita (1988).

60. Feinberg, Joel (1985), p. 34.

61. Any item of clothing can be substituted here.

62. VanDeVeer, Donald (1979).

63. Ibid., p. 182.

64. An example may be the reaction a person has to the sight of blood or rotting flesh.

65. Feinberg, Joel (1985), p. 36.
66. In this case such offense was, probably, based on the view that women are not as intelligent as men. Through testing and other forms of evaluation, this view can be demonstrated to be false. Given this falsity, the offense is unreasonable.
67. Feinberg, Joel (1985), pp. 36–37.
68. Ibid., p. 37.
69. Unsolicited e-mail sent to multiple accounts.
70. Graham, Gordon (1999), p. 121.

Chapter 7

1. I have not yet found any arguments that are more convincing.
2. I do not wish to imply here that autonomy is somehow intrinsically valuable. While in most moral philosophy it has emerged as somewhat of a super value, I do not believe that one can merely assume that it is, However, I believe that it is safe to say is that it is valued and possesses at least instrumental value. Given this, it would create injury if impeded.
3. Mill, John Stuart (1969), p. 256.
4. It has been claimed that Mill's discussion of liberty as a right is inconsistent with his commitments to Utilitarianism. While I believe that his commitment to liberty can be justified by an indirect form of consequentalism, it is not directly relevant to my purposes here.
5. Mill, John Stuartm (1991), p. 17.
6. Does not harm others,
7. There is some evidence that Mill thought that even self-regarding actions could be harmful; see Jacobson, Daniel (2000).
8. Mill's corn-dealer example is a case where he believes regulation is appropriate based on the severity of the likely outcomes.
9. Feinberg, Joel (1973), p. 21.
10. While the scope of this vast harm is limited to places where freedom is valued, it does not suffer many problems that some rights- and autonomy-based justifications have encountered. Some of these problems include justifying the intrinsic value of autonomy and meeting utilitarian challenges to rights-based theories.
11. Locke, John (1960), p. 287.
12. While this may be a just violation, it is still a breach of the right.
13. It should be noted that a "right" has been defined in many ways. A few theorists claim that rights are absolute; however, most take a less severe stance and claim that rights are "side constraints" or "trumps."
14. Many authors in the classical liberal or libertarian tradition make arguments similar to this.
15. See Dworkin, Ronald (1977) and (1985).
16. Rawls, John (1971).
17. Lomasky, Loren (1987).
18. Gewirth, Alan (1984), pp. 91–109.
19. A negative consequence produced.
20. Tisdale, Sallie (1992), p. 45.
21. Gardiner, Judith Kegan (1993).
22. United States Department of Justice (1986), p. 1028.
23. Strossen, Nadine (1995), p. 163.
24. Candida Royalle of Femme Productions produces films for this purpose.
25. It should be noted that I am not a technophile and do not wish to advance the position that all new technology is inherently valuable. However, only a neoluddite would fail to see that many newer technologies have improved the quality of life for many persons.
26. Johnson, Peter (1998).
27. Hunt, Lynn (1993), pp. 9–18.
28. Goffman, Erving (1959).
29. Quoted in de Grazia, Edward (1992), p. 671.
30. Diamond, Sara (1985), p. 57.
31. MacKinnon, Catharine (1989), p. 202.

32. Bentley, Chris (1992).

33. Hentoff, Nat (1991).

34. Strossen, Nadine (1995).

35. Ibid., 226.

36. In the small town in which I reside a public meeting was recently held to oppose the teaching of sexual education in the high school.

37. *ACLU v. Reno,* 929 F. Supp. 824, 857 (E.D.pa 1996) aff'd, 521 U.S. 844 (1997).

38. Populations of persons with alternative sexual orientations and/or a minority ethnicity.

39. Strossen, Nadine (1995), p. 219.

40. Ibid., p. 55.

41. Quoted in de Grazia, Edward (1992), p. 622.

42. Strossen, Nadine (1995), pp. 169–170.

43. Ibid., p. 232.

44. Ibid., p. 265.

45. Ted Bundy and Thomas Schiro are two examples.

46. In fact, in *Only Words,* Catharine MacKinnon argues that pornography destroyed Thomas Schiro's ability to understand that the brutal rape and torturous murder he committed were wrong. Because of this, MacKinnon believes Schiro should have been pardoned; see MacKinnon, Catharine (1993), pp. 95–97.

47. Graham, Gordon (1999).

48. Ibid., p. 2.

49. Volokh, Eugene (1995).

50. Graham, Gordon (1999), pp. 37–38.

51. A term used to designate E-bay users whose main source of income comes from selling items using E-bay online auctions.

52. Internet Relay Chat

53. Reid, Elizabeth (1991).

54. A website (or section of one) where users can post a chronological, up-to-date e-journal entry of their thoughts.

55. Lessig, Lawrence (2003), p. 136.

56. Ibid.

57. Unfortunately it was not popular enough to win Dean the democratic nomination.

58. An electronic bulletin board system.

59. Rheingold, Howard (1993), Chapter 4.

60. Ibid.

61. Ibid.

62. Ibid.

63. Ibid.

64. Ibid., Chapter 6.

65. Rheingold's latest work, *Smart Mobs: The Next Social Revolution,* examines the newest linkage methods involving handheld devices and the social implications thereof.

66. *R. v. Butler,* 1 S.C.R. 452 (1992). In this case it was decided that sexually explicit materials that contain violence and/or are degrading should be considered obscene and regulated.

67. Human Rights Watch Free Expression Project, *A Ruling Inspired by U.S. Pornography Activists Is Used to Restrict Lesbian and Gay Publications in Canada,* February 1994, 8–9.

68. Ibid., 8

69. Slevin, James (2000).

70. One of the main justifications given in the *Butler* decision was that sexually explicit materials are degrading to women.

71. Scott, Sarah (1993).

72. Kingston, Tim (1993).

73. Heins, Majorie (1993), pp. 61–63.

74. Strossen, Nadine (1995), p. 239.

75. *United States v. American Library Association* (02–361), 23 June 2003.

76. Please note that I do not object to filters being utilized by individuals who wish to use them and are willing to accept the costs involved.

77. Electronic Privacy Information Center (2000), pp. 29–30.

78. Ibid., p. 30.

79. Everard, Jerry (2000).

80. Graham, Gordon (1999), p. 93.

81. While, thus far, the Internet has quite an impressive record for escaping governmental control, it is possible that, in order to block access to pornography and obscenity, regulation would be so stringent that this power to bypass governmental controls would be severely weakened.

82. Graham, Gordon (1999), p. 93.

83. To be effective, e-mail would need to be regulated because pornography and obscenity can easily be sent over e-mail.

84. I believe this is true even with the currant panic concerning terrorism in the United States.

85. *Reason* ran an article discussing the impact of the crackdown on Oxy-Contin. This article argued that the crackdown has restricted the ability of physicians to prescribe needed pain medications; see Ammann, Melinda (2003), pp. 28–34.

86. Platt, Charles (1996), pp. 22–36.

87. Cyber Patrol allows persons to choose what programs can be used while Net Nanny and Zone Alarm Pro allow users to block access to many popular file-sharing programs.

88. Saaf, Randy, Written Testimony for the Oversight Hearing on the prevalence of Pornography, Including Child Pornography, on Peer-to-Peer Networks, United States Congress, 13 March 2003.

89. This is assuming the use of current or similar programming languages to construct such filters. While it is possible that a radically different design built on a new language will come about, it is highly unlikely given what we know about the limitations of computing ability.

90. The development of this new filtering technology was brought to my attention in a discussion at the Computers and Philosophy (CAP) conference in January of 2001. I am grateful to CAP participants at the 2001 and 2003 conferences for informing me of recent developments regarding this technology.

Bibliography

Addicted to Noise. (1999.) "Senators Equate Hazards of Music, Film, Video Games with Tobacco." Accessed on 1 January 2006 at http://www.massmic.com/warninglabel.html.

Aftab, Parry. (2000.) *The Parent's Guide to Protecting Your Children in Cyberspace*. New York: McGraw-Hill.

Alexander, Gregory S. (1989.) "Dilemmas of Group Autonomy: Residential Association and Community." *Cornell Law Review*, 75, 17–23.

Alston, Richard. (2000.) "The Government's Regulatory Framework for Internet Content." *University of New South Wales Law Journal Forum*, 6 (1), 45.

Ambah, Faiza. (1995.) "An Intruder in the Kingdom." *Business Week*, 21 August, 40.

Ammann, Melinda. (2003.) "The Agony and the Ecstasy." *Reason*, April, 28–34.

Anderson, Ray. (1999.) "The Pornography Question: Main Event or Sideshow?" I James Elias (ed.), *Porn 101: Eroticism, Pornography, and the First Amendment*. Amherst, NY: Prometheus Books, pp. 219–222.

Aries, Philippe. (1962.) *Centuries of Childhood*. New York: Vintage.

Attorney General's Commission on Pornography. (1986.) *Final Report*. Washington, DC: U.S. Government Printing Office.

Barlow, John Perry. (1995.) "Is There a There in Cyberspace?" *Utne Reader,* March–April, 53–56.

Baron, L. (1990.) "Feminist Perspectives on Sexuality." *Journal of Sex Research,* 27 363–380.

BBC. (2002.) "China Blocking Google." *BBC News.* Accessed on 10 March 2006 at http://news.bbc.co.uk/1/hi/technology/2231101.stm.

Bentley, Chris. (1992.) "Mall Nixes Artwork as Shocking." *News-Leader* (Springfield MO), 5 March.

Berger, Fred. (1977.) "Pornography, Sex, and Censorship." *Social Theory and Practice,* 4 (2), 183–209.

Bertin, Joan. (1998.)"Views on the News from the Executive Director: National Coalition Against Censorship." *Censorship News,* Winter.

Bickel, Alexander. (1971.) "On Pornography: Dissenting and Concurring Opinions." *Public Interest*, 25, 25–26.

Bogert, Carole. (1995.) "Chat Rooms and Chadors." *Newsweek,* 21 August, 36.

Bollinger, Lee. (1980.) *The Tolerant Society.* New York: Oxford University Press.

Bork, Robert. (1997.) *Slouching towards Gomorrah.* New York: Regan Books.

169

Brod, Harry. (1988.) "Pornography and the Alienation of Male Sexuality." *Social Theory and Practice*, 14 (3), 114–121.

Buckley, William. (1998.) "You Figure It Out." In Robert Baird and Stuart Rosenblum (eds.), *Pornography: Private Right or Public Menace?* Amherst, NY: Prometheus, pp. 63–65.

Burger, Robert H. (1987.) "The Meese Report on Pornography and Its Respondents: A Review Article." *Library Quarterly*, 57, 436–447.

Burges, Johnson. (1948.) *The Lost Art of Profanity.* Indianapolis: Bobbs-Merrill.

Buruma, Ian. A. (1984.) *Japanese Mirror: Heroes and Villains of Japanese Culture.* London: Penguin.

Carter, D. I., et al. (1987.) "Use of Pornography in the Criminal and Developmental Histories of Sexual Offenders." *Journal of Interpersonal Violence*, 2, 196–211.

Christensen, F. M. (1990.) *Pornography: The Other Side.* New York: Praeger.

Cohen, Bram. (2005.) "Incentives Build Robustness in BitTorrent." Accessed on 14 December 2005 at http://www.bittorrent.com/bittorrentecon.pdf.

Cohen, Myer. (1937.) *Selected Supreme Court Decisions.* New York: Harper and Brothers.

Committee to Study Tools and Strategies for Protecting Kids from Pornography and Their Applicability to Other Inappropriate Internet Content. (2002.) *Youth Pornography and the Internet.* Dick Thornburgh and Herbert S. Lin (eds..) Washington, DC: National Academy Press, p. 74.

Comstock, Anthony. (1967.) *Traps for the Young.* Cambridge, MA: Belknap Press.

Cotler, Irwin. (2000.) "Holocaust Denial, Equality, and Harm: Boundaries of Liberty and Tolerance in a Liberal Democracy." In Raphael Cohen-Almagor (ed.), *Liberal Democracy and the Limits of Tolerance.* Ann Arbor: University of Michigan Press.

Cox, Phil. (1997.) "The Conceits of Law and the Transmission of the Indecent, Obscene and Ugly." *Journal of Information Ethics*, 6 (2), 23–34.

Davidson, Sandra, and Betty Houchin Winfield. (1999.) *Bleep: Censoring Rock and Rap Music.* Westport, CT: Greenwood Press.

De Grazia, Edward. (1992.) *Girls Lean Back Everywhere: The Law of Obscenity and the Assault on Genius.* New York: Vintage Books.

Devlin, Patrick. (1959.) *The Enforcement of Morals.* Oxford: Oxford University Press.

Diamond, Milton, and Uchiyama, Ayako. (1999.) "Pornography, Rape and Other Sex Crimes in Japan." *International Journal of Law and Psychiatry*, 22, 1, 5.

Diamond, Sara. (1985.) "Pornography: Image and Reality." In Varda Burstyn (ed.), *Women against Censorship.* Vancouver: Douglas and McIntyre, p. 57.

Dibbell, Julian. (1996.) "A Rape in Cyberspace: How an Evil Clown, a Haitian Trickster Spirit, Two Wizards, and a Cast of Dozens Turned a Database into a Society." In Mark Stefik (ed.), *Internet Dreams: Archetypes, Myths and Metaphors.* Cambridge, MA: MIT Press, pp. 293–296.

Dority, Barbara. (1989.) "Feminist Moralism, Pornography, and Censorship." *Humanist*, 8–9 (46), 151.

Dworkin, Andrea. (1979.) *Pornography: Men Possessing Women.* New York: E.P. Dutton.

Dworkin, Andrea. (1993.) *Letters from a War Zone.* New York: Lawrence Hill Books.

Dworkin, Andrea, and Catharine MacKinnon. (1988.) *Pornography and Civil Rights: A New Day for Women's Equality.* Minneapolis: Organizing against Pornography.

Dworkin, Ronald. (1977.) *Taking Rights Seriously.* London: Ducksworth.

Dworkin, Ronald. (1985.) *A Matter of Principle.* Cambridge, MA: Harvard University Press.

Elgin, Ben, and Bruce Einhorn. (2006.) "The Great Firewall of China." *Businessweek Online,* 12 January. Accessed 13 January 2006 at http://www.bussinessweek.com.

Elias, James. (1999.) "Great War Stories: Warriors and Their Battles over Obscenity." In Elias, James (ed.), *Porn 101: Eroticism, Pornography, and the First Amendment.* Amherst, NY: Prometheus, p. 31.

Electronic Privacy Information Center. (2000.) *Filters and Freedom: Perspectives on Internet Content Controls.* Washington, DC: Electronic Privacy Information Center.

Ely, J. (1980.) *Democracy and Distrust.* Cambridge, MA: Harvard University Press.

Eron, L. D., and L. R. Huesmann. (1980.) "Adolescent Aggression and Television." *Annals of the New York Academy of Sciences,* 347, 319–331.

Everard, Jerry. (2000.) *Virtual States: The Internet and the Boundaries of the Nation-State.* New York: Routledge.

Exon, Jim. (1998.) "Commentary: The Communications Decency Act." In Robert Baird (ed.), *Pornography: Private Right or Public Menace?* Amherst, NY: Prometheus, pp. 46–48.

Falk, Jim. (1998.) "The Meaning of the Web." *Information and Society,* 14, 285–289.

Feinberg, Joel. (1973.) *Social Philosophy.* Englewood Cliffs, NJ: Prentice-Hall.

Feinberg, Joel. (1980.) "Harmless Immoralities and Offensive Nuisances." In *Rights, Liberty and the Bounds of Justice.* Princeton: Princeton University Press.

Feinberg, Joel. (1984.) *Harm to Others.* Oxford: Oxford University Press.

Feinberg, Joel. (1985.) *Offense to Others.* New York: Oxford University Press.

Feinberg, Joel. (1992.) "Limits to the Free Expression of Opinion." In *Freedom and Fulfillment: Philosophical Essays.* Princeton: Princeton University Press.

Fischer, W. A. (1994.) "Violent Pornography, Antiwomen Thoughts, and Antiwomen Acts: In Search of Reliable Effects." *Journal of Sex Research,* 31, 23–38.

Ford, M. E, and J. A. Linney. (1995.) "Comparative Analysis of Juvenile Sexual Offenders, and Status Offenders." *Journal of Interpersonal Violence,* 10, 56–76.

Friedman, Samuel Joshua. (2000.) *Children and the World Wide Web.* Lanham, MD: University Press of America.

Gardiner, Judith Kegan. (1993.) "What I Didn't Get to Say about Pornography, Masculinity, and Repression." *New York Law Review,* 38, 319–333.

Gay, Peter. (1984.) *The Bourgeois Experience: Victoria to Freud.* Vol. 2, *Education of the Senses.* New York: Oxford University Press.

Gelder, Lindsay Van. (1985.) "The Strange Case of the Electronic Lover." *Ms.,* October.

Gellhorn, Walter. (1956.) *Individual Freedom and Governmental Restraint.* Baton Rouge: Louisiana State University Press.

George, Robert P. (1993.) *Making Men Moral: Civil Liberties and Public Morality.* Oxford: Clarendon Press.

Gewirth, Alan. (1984.) "Are There Any Absolute Rights?" In Jeremy Waldron (ed.), *Theories of Right.,* Oxford: Oxford University Press, pp. 91–109.

Godwin, Mike. (1995.) "The Electronic Frontier Foundation and Virtual Communities." Accessed on 10 March 2006 at http://www.eff.org/Misc/Publications/Mike_Godwin/virtual_communities.eff.

Goffman, Erving. (1959.) *The Presentation of Self in Everyday Life.* New York: Doubleday.

Gore, Tipper. (1987.) *Raising PG Kids in an X-rated Society.* Nashville, TN: Parthenon Press.

Graham, Gordon. (1999.) *The Internet: A Philosophical Inquiry.* New York: Routledge.

Hafferkamp, Jack. (1999.) "Un-Banning Books: How the Courts of the United States Came to Extend First Amendment Guarantees to Include Pornography." In James Elias (ed.), *Porn 101.* Amherst, NY: Prometheus.

Hafner, Katie. (1997.) "The Epic Saga of the Well." *Wired,* May, 98.

Hart, H. L. A. (1963.) *Law, Liberty, and Morality.* Stanford, CA: Stanford University Press.

Hayward, S., and R. Batcheider. (2001.) "Peer-to-Peer: Something Old, Something New." *Gartner,* 10 April.

Heins, Majorie. (1993.) *Sex, Sin and Blasphemy.* New York: New York Press, pp. 92–99.

Heins, Majorie. (1995.) "*American Civil Liberties Union v. ACLU*: The 1996 Communications Decency Act." In James Elias (ed.), *Porn 101.* Amherst, NY: Prometheus.

Hentoff, Nat. (1990.) "The Constitutionalist." *The New Yorker,* 12 March, 56.

Hentoff, Nat. (1991.) "Sexual Harassment by Francisco Goya." *Washington Post,* 27 December, A1.

Hill, Judith. (1998.) "Pornography and Degradation." In Robert Baird (ed.), *Pornography: Private Right or Public Menace?* Amherst, NY: Prometheus, pp. 100–113.

Howitt, D. (1995.) "Pornography and the Pedophile: Is It Criminogenic?" *British Journal of Medical Psychology,* 68, 5–27.

Huelster, Pamela. (1995.) "Cybersex and Community Standards." *Boston University Law Review,* 75, May.

Hunt, Lynn. (1994.) *The Invention of Pornography.* New York: Zone Books.

Intons-Peterson, M. J., et al. (1989.) "Will Educational Materials Reduce Negative Effects of Exposure to Sexual Violence?" *Journal of Social and Clinical Psychology,* 8, 256–275.

Jacobson, Daniel. (2000.) "Mill on Liberty, Speech and the Free Society." *Philosophy and Public Affairs,* 29.

Jaffe, J. Michael. (2000.) "Riding the Electronic Tiger: Censorship in Global Distributed Networks." In Cohen-Almagor, Raphael (ed.), *Liberal Democracy and the Limits of Tolerance.* Ann Arbor: University of Michigan Press.

Jefferson, Thomas. (1999.) *Thomas Jefferson's Garden Book.* Edwin Morris (ed..) Betts, VA: Thomas Jefferson Memorial Foundation.

Johnson, Peter. (1998.) "Pornography Drives Technology." In Robert Baird (ed.), *Pornography: Private Right or Public Menace?* Amherst, NY: Prometheus. Kaplan, Dawn. (1998.) "Cyber-smut: Regulating Obscenity on the Internet." *Stanford Law and Policy Review,* 9, 189–195.

Kendrick, Walter. (1987.) *The Secret Museum: Pornography in Modern Culture.* New York: Viking.

Kingston, Tim. (1993.) "Canada's New Porn Wars: 'Little Sister' Gay/Lesbian Bookstore Battles Canadian Customs." *San Francisco Bay Times,* 4 November.

Knoll, Amy. (1996.) "Any Which Way But Loose: Nations Regulate the Internet." *Tulane Journal of International and Comparative Law,* 275 (Summer): 275.

Knudsen, D. D. (1988.) "Child Sexual Abuse and Pornography: Is There a Relationship?" *Journal of Family Violence,* 3, 253–267.

Kurland, Philip B. (1975.) *Free Speech and Association: The Supreme Court and the First Amendment.* Chicago: University of Chicago Press.

Kutchinsky, B. (1991.) "Pornography and Rape: Theory and Practice? Evidence from Crime Data in Four Countries: Pornography Is Easily Available." *International Journal of Law Psychology*, 26, 47–64.

Kuthchinsky, B. (1973.) "The Effect of Easy Availability of Pornography on the Incidence of Sex Crimes: The Danish Experience." *Journal of Social Issues*, 29, 163–181.

Langevin, R., and R. A. Lang. (1985.) "Psychological Treatment of the Pedophile." *Behavioral Sciences and the Law*, 3, 403–419.

Langevin, R., et al. (1988.) "Pornography and Sexual Offenses." *Annual of Sex Research*, 1, 335–362.

Langton, Rae. (1993.) "Speech Acts and Unspeakable Acts." *Philosophy and Public Affairs*, 22 (4), 292–330.

Layhaye, Tim. (1998.) "The Mental Poison." In Robert Baird (ed.), *Pornography: Private Right or Public Menace?* Amherst, NY: Prometheus, pp. 202–214.

Lessig, Lawrence. (2003.) "The New Road to the White House." *Wired*, 2 November, 36.

Linsley, William. (1998.) "The Case against Censorship of Pornography." In Robert Baird (ed.), *Pornography: Private Right or Public Menace?* Amherst, NY: Prometheus, pp. 176–190.

Lloyd, Margaret A., and Wayne Weiten. (1994.) *Psychology Applied to Modern Life.* Pacific Grove, CA: Brooks/Cole.

Locke, John. (1960.) "The Second Treatise of Government: An Essay Concerning the True Original, Extent, and End of Civil Government." In Peter Laslett (ed.), *Two Treatises of Government.* Cambridge: Cambridge University Press.

Lomasky, Loren. (1987.) *Persons, Rights, and the Moral Community.* New York: Oxford University Press.

Longino, Helen E. (1998.) "Pornography, Oppression and Freedom: A Closer Look." In Robert Baird (ed.), *Pornography: Private Right or Public Menace?* Amherst, NY: Prometheus, pp. 122–133.

Loundy, David. (1994.) "Whose Standards? Whose Community?" *Chicago Daily Law Bulletin*, 1 August, 5.

Lunsford, Brock. (1997.) "Current Developments in the Law: *United States v. Thomas.*" *Boston Public Internet Law Journal*, 805.

MacKinnon, Catharine. (1989.) *Toward a Feminist Theory of the State.* Cambridge, MA: Harvard University Press.

MacKinnon, Catharine. (1993.) *Only Words.* Cambridge, MA: Harvard University Press.

MacKinnon, Catharine A. (1985.) "Pornography, Civil Rights, and Speech." *Harvard. Civil Rights — Civil Liberties Law Review*, 20, 1–70.

Malamuth, N. M., and J. P. Check. (1981.) "The Effects of Media Exposure on Acceptance of Violence against Women: A Field Experiment." *Journal of Research in Personality*, 15, 436–446.

Manning, Rita. (1994.) "Redefining Obscenity." *Journal of Value Inquiry*, 22, 193–205.

Martin, Mitchell. (1995.) "Germany Forces CompuServe to Censor Sex on the Internet." *International Herald Tribune*, 29 December.

McLaughlin, Mary Martin. (1974.) "Survivors and Surrogates: Children and Parents from the Ninth to the Thirteenth Centuries." In Lloyd de Mause (ed.), *The History of Childhood.* New York: Psychohistory Press.

McPhee, Mike. (1998.) "Oregon Man Held in Internet Sex Sting." *Denver Post,* 14 February, B-03.

Meiklejohn, Alexander. (1948.) *Free Speech and Its Relation to Self-Government.* New York: Harper.

Mein, C. T. (1995.) "Lee Kuan Says Yes to Internet, No to Sex and Violence on TV." *Agence France Presse,* 6 October, 35.

Michael, Jennifer. (1997.) "Obscenity: Where's 'The Nastiest Place on Earth?' From Roth to Cyberspace, or, Whose Community Is It, Anyway?" *Creighton Law Review,* 20 (June): 1405.

Michener, Andrew, and John D. Delamater. (1994.) *Social Psychology.* Orlando, FL: Harcount and Brace.

Mill, John Stuart. (1969.) *The Collected Works of John Stuart Mill.* J. M. Robson (ed..) Toronto: University of Toronto Press.

Mill, John Stuart. (1969.) *On Liberty; Representative Government; The Subjection of Women.* London: Oxford University Press.

Mill, John Stuart. (1991.) *On Liberty and Other Essays* (1859.) New York: Oxford University Press.

Mintz, Anne. (2000.) *Web of Deception: Misinformation and the Internet.* Medford, NJ: CyberAge Books.

Mintz, Howard. (1995.) "Offensive to Professional Standards: The Appeal of a Milpitas Couple's Computer Pornography Conviction Focuses Far More on the Trial Counsel's Performance Than the 1st Amendment." *Recorder,* 5 January.

Moore, Dinty W. (1995.) *The Emperor's Virtual Cloths: The Naked Truth about Internet Culture.* Chapel Hill, NC: Algonquin Books.

Myers, David. (1992.) *Psychology.* 3rd ed. Holland, MI: Worth.

Negropointe, Nicholas. (1991.) "Products and Services for Computer Networks." *Scientific American,* September, 76.

Orwell, George. (1949.) *Nineteen Eighty-Four.* New York: Harcourt.

Padgett, V. R., et al. (1989.) "Pornography, Erotica, and Attitudes towards Women: The Effects of Repeated Exposure." *Journal of Sex Research,* 26, 479–491.

Pagels, Elaine. (1988.) *Adam, Eve and the Serpent.* New York: Vintage.

Pally, Marcia. (1994.) *Sex and Sensibility: Reflections on Forbidden Mirrors and the Will to Censor.* Hopewell, NJ: Ecco Press.

Parke, R. D., et al. (1964.) "Some Effects of Violent and Nonviolent Movies on the Behavior of Juvenile Delinquents." In Leonard Berkowitz (ed.), *Advances in Experimental Social Psychology.* New York: Academic Press.

Pateman, Carole. (1988.) *The Sexual Contract,* Stanford, CA: Stanford University Press.

Patterson, G. R., et al. (1991.) "A Comparative Evaluation of Parent Training Procedures." *Behavior Therapy,* 13, 638–650.

Petrie, Sean. (1997.) "Indecent Proposals: How Each Branch of the Federal Government Overstepped Its Institutional Authority in the Development of Internet Obscenity Law." *Stanford Law Review,* 49, 637.

Plagen, Peter. (1991.) "Violence in Our Culture." *Newsweek,* 1 April, 1, 46.

Platt, Charles. (1996.) *Anarchy Online.* New York: HarperPrism.

Poole, Howard. (1982.) "Obscenity and Censorship." *Ethics* 3 (1), 39–44.

Postman, Neil. (1986.) *Amusing Ourselves to Death: Public Discourse in the Age of Show Business.* New York: Penguin Books.

Rauch, Jonathan. (1998.) "New Threats to Free Thought." In Richard Stichler and

Robert Hauptman (eds.), *Freedom of Information and the Pursuit of Knowledge*. NC: McFarland.

Rawls, John. (1971.) *A Theory of Justice*. Cambridge, MA: Harvard University Press.

Reid, Elizabeth. (1991.) "Electropolis: Communication and Community on Internet Relay Chat." Honours Thesis, University of Melbourne. Accessed 12 September 2003 at http://home.earthlink.net/~aluluei/ecectropolis.htm.

Reuters. (2002.) "Google Inaccessible in China." *CNET News.co*. Accessed 21 January 2006 at http://news.com.com/2100–1023–956243.html.

Rheingold, Howard. (1993.) *The Virtual Community*. Accessed 22 January 2006 at http://www.rheingold.com/vc/book/.

Rich, Frank. (2001.) "Naked Capitalists: There's No Business Like Porn Business." *New York Times Magazine*, 20 May.

Royalle, Candida. (1993.) "Porn in the USA." *Social Text*, Winter, 23–35.

Ripenau, Matel, et al. (2002.) "Mapping the Gnutella Network: Properties of Large Scale Peer-to-Peer Systems and Implication for System Design." *IEEE Internet Computing*, 6 (1.)

Scanlon, Thomas. (1972.) "A Theory of Freedom of Expression." *Philosophy and Public Affairs*, 1, 204–226.

Scanlon, Thomas M. (1979.) "Freedom of Expression and Categories of Expression." *University of Pittsburgh Law Review*, 40.

Schauer, Fredrick. (1976.) *The Law of Obscenity*. Washington, DC: Bureau of National Affairs.

Schauer, Fredrick. (1982.) *Free Speech: A Philosophical Enquiry*. Cambridge: Cambridge University Press.

Scotland. National Offender Management Service Home Office. (2005.) *Consultation: On the Possession of Extreme Pornographic Material*. Accessed on 21 January 2006 at http://www.homeoffice.gov.uk/documents/cons-extreme-porn-300805.

Scott, Sarah. (1993.) "Porn Police: Who Decides What to Ban at the Border." *Montreal Gazette*, 14 April.

Slevin, James (2000.) *The Internet and Society*. Malden, MA: Polity Press.

Smith, Steve. (2005.) "The Changing Face of BitTorrent: Is BT the Next HTTP?" *Computer Power User*, 5 November, 79–80.

Smith, Tom W. (1987.) "The Use of Public Opinion Data by the Attorney General's Commission on Pornography." *Public Opinion Quarterly*, 51 (2), 249–267.

Smolla, Rodney A. (1992.) *Free Speech in an Open Society*. New York: Alfred Knopf.

Steinem, Gloria. (1998.) "Erotica and Pornography: A Clear and Present Difference." In Robert Baird (ed.), *Pornography: Private Right or Public Menace?* Amherst, NY: Prometheus, pp. 89–93.

Strossen, Nadine. (1995.) *Defending Pornography: Free Speech, Sex and the Fight for Women's Rights*. New York: Scribner's.

Strossen, Nadine (1998.) "Academic and Artistic Freedom." In Richard Stichler and Robert Hauptman (eds.), *Freedom of Information and the Pursuit of Knowledge*. Jefferson, NC: McFarland, 1998.

Tanenbaum, Leora. (1994.) "Politics of Porn: Forced Arguments."*In These Time*s, 7 March, 18.

Tisdale, Sallie. (1992.) "Talk Dirty to Me: A Woman's Taste for Pornography." *Harper's*, February, 45.

Tissot, Samueal-Auguste. (1766.) *A Treatise on the Crime of Onan*. 3rd ed. London: B. Thomas.

Thornburgh, Dick, and Herbert Lin (eds.). (2002.) *Youth, Pornography and the Internet*. Washington, DC: National Academy Press.

Tyler, R. P., and L. E. Stone. (1985.) "Child Pornography: Perpetuating the Sexual Victimization of Children: Fifth International Congress on Child Abuse and Neglect." *Child Abuse and Neglect*, 13–18.

United States Department of Justice. (1986.) *Attorney General's Commission on Pornography, Final Report*. Washington, DC: U.S. GPO.

United States. Congress. (2003.) *Stumbling onto Smut: The Alarming Ease of Access to Pornography on Peer-to-Peer Network*. Hearing before the Committee on Government Reform. House of Representatives,108st Congress, 1st Sess. Washington, DC: GPO.

VanDeVeer, Donald. (1979.) "Coercive Restraint of Offensive Actions." *Philosophy and Public Affairs*, 8 (2), 175–195.

Veyne, Paul. (1987.) "The Roman Empire." In P. Aries and G. Duby (eds.), *A History of Private Life*. Vol. 1, *From Pagan Rome to Byzantium*. Cambridge, MA: Harvard University Press,

Volokh, Eugene. (1995.) "Emerging Media Technology and the First Amendment: Cheap Speech and What It Will Do." *Yale Law Journal*, 104 (May): 1639.

Wallace, Jonathan,. and Mark Mangan. (1997.) *Sex Laws and Cyberspace*. New York: Henry Holt.

Warning, Sarah. (2002.) "NU Pressured to Crack Down on File Sharing on Computers." *Daily Northwestern*, 25 October.

White, Harry. (1997.) *Anatomy of Censorship: Why the Censors Have It Wrong*. New York: University Press of America.

Wilcox, Brian L. (1987.) "Pornography, Social Science, and Politics: When Research and Ideology Collided." *American Psychologist*, 42, 941–943.

Willard, Nancy. (1997.) *The Cyberethics Reader*. New York: McGraw-Hill.

Will, George F. (1990.) "America's Slide into the Sewer." *Newsweek,* 30 July.

Wolk, Martin. (2006.) "Search Giant Battle Bolsters Reputation on Privacy Rights." *MSNBC Online*. Accessed 15 February 2006 at http:// www.msnbc.msn.com.

Index